Philip Johnson
The Architect in His Own Words

Philip Johnson
The Architect in His Own Words

**Hilary Lewis
and John O'Connor**

RIZZOLI
NEW YORK

First published in the United States of America in 1994 by
Rizzoli International Publications, Inc.
300 Park Avenue South, New York, New York 10010

Library of Congress Cataloging-in-Publication Data
Johnson, Philip, 1906–
      Philip Johnson: the architect in his own words / Hilary
Lewis and John O'Connor
            p. cm.
      Includes bibliographical references.
      ISBN 0-8478-1823-3
      1. Johnson, Philip, 1906– —Interviews. 2. Architects—
United States—Interviews. 3. Architecture, Modern—20th
century—United States. I. Lewis, Hilary, 1962– .
II. O'Connor, John T. (John Timothy) III. Title.
NA737.J6A35 1994
720'.92—dc·20   94-16057
                                                          CIP

Design by John O'Connor
Printed and bound in Italy

Is not life a hundred times too short to bore ourselves?

Friedrich Wilhelm Nietzsche
Beyond Good and Evil 1886

There is only one thing in the world worse than being talked about, and that is not being talked about.

Oscar Wilde
The Picture of Dorian Gray 1891

Contents

Philip Johnson is a complex character who today, at 88, envelops a multitude of artistic personas. He is like the sharp-witted photographer Weegee — snapping candid photos of Cambridge matrons on their hands and knees trying to peek under the wall surrounding his Ash Street home. He is the detail-obsessed counterpart to Mies van der Rohe, insisting on no bedside reading lamp in the Glass House. "It would spoil the effect," says Johnson. "Effect before everything." And like his late friend Andy Warhol, he is an outspoken celebrity who likes to confuse the critics and leave the public wondering, "Is he serious?" He has moved beyond his "architect as whore" quote just as Warhol defused his "15 minutes of fame" edict by countering, "In 15 minutes, everyone will be famous."

These traits keep Johnson from being pinned down, keep him constantly innovating, dissolving rules, and perhaps most importantly, give him a superb sense of humor. This is exceptional in a field that is often seen as deadly serious — to the point where architects, customarily sheathed in black, appear to be nothing if not bereft.

Johnson is the controversial mad scientist of his profession. Always an experimenter, Johnson and his work seem to expand the envelope in ways that often put the field on edge. Why not adapt Brunelleschi's Renaissance windows for use in a small brick guest house? What's wrong with admiring the inmate-surveillance qualities of a jail — and applying them at Lincoln Center? Johnson is always willing to make that intuitive leap from which other architects may shy away.

Johnson references the gamut and is able to admire the fastidious gardens of Le Nôtre as well as the super grandeur and camp of Morris Lapidus's Miami Beach hotels. Johnson refuses to acknowledge what others see as his foible: an historian's background combined with a pop sensibility. For this his work is enshrined by some, decried by others. But to Johnson, it's all Monday-morning quarterbacking. Retrospective criticism is too easy: maybe they're right, maybe not. He's too busy creating to look back right now. Look at the work, he seems to say, you decide what holds it all together. Like he says of Frank Lloyd Wright, Johnson himself seems to be "much more all over the place than one talks about." The architect seems to cover the last half-century in a panoply of styles.

However, if one looks closely, his work reveals a common thread. Encompassing the minimalist look of the Glass House and the modern night-on-the-town glamour of the New York State Theater as well as the deconstructivist qualities of International Place in Boston, the buildings of Johnson, and later Johnson and Burgee, reflect the time of their construction exactly — and usually before anyone can recognize it. Some of the works are today regarded as museum pieces.

In the late 1970s, while cities around the globe were erecting bastardizations of International Style office towers, Johnson and Burgee were finishing a granite clad, goldleafed, postmodern masterwork for AT&T. The practice of reviving history for use in a new movement had earlier emerged in the forms of smaller buildings, but it took Johnson — never afraid of the marriage of art and commerce — to put it firmly on the map. At the time, critics panned the AT&T Building for its broken pediment roofline and Piranesian-scaled entrance. It now is seen as the turning point in a movement that revived decorative programs of expression and the art of building corporate symbols, something not seen in full force since the time of Chicago's Tribune Tower competition in 1922.

More to the point, it clearly represents its place in time — the 1980s, the years of corporate takeovers, multimillion dollar salaries, and be-

ANDY WARHOL WITH PHILIP JOHNSON IN 1979

jeweled ballgowns. The following decade would see a virtual stampede for the trappings of wealth and prestige. Corporations begged for their own identifiable symbols of permanence. The public sector discarded Formica and Farberware for granite and Michael Graves-designed teapots. But before the stock market crash of 1987, before postmodernism became as symbolic of self-indulgence as the discovery of Imelda Marcos's shoe collection, Johnson was again getting restless. By then he had for the most part dropped the fountained courts and gilded trappings of a movement at its height of acceptance to focus on the naked geometry, disturbing angles, and cheaper materials of a nascent movement called deconstructivism.

Like house cats in Los Angeles before an earthquake, he and a few other architects feel the first signs of an impending shift — not only an architectural movement but perhaps a societal sea change as well. Johnson explains his disappointment with a client's decision to complete the more traditional of his two designs for an office center in Berlin. "They have every right to say what they want. But this seemed kind of sad to me when the context of the site was just a rock. . . . I say you've got to have something of our time." Something of our time.

Exactly.

John O'Connor
Cambridge, Massachusetts, 1994

We approached Philip Johnson about participating in this book in 1992, not long after he had, at age 86, begun yet another chapter in his lengthy career by opening his current firm, Philip Johnson Architects. Johnson, who appears to know almost no limits due to age, works full-time from his office in the so-called Lipstick building in New York. All of the conversations in the following chapters took place in that office between 1992 and 1994.

We want to note that from 1967 through 1989, Johnson worked with the firm of Johnson/Burgee (later John Burgee Architects), and during the 1950s and 1960s, he worked in partnership with Richard Foster. In fact, for most of Johnson's career he has worked with associated architects. We do not mean to ignore the contributions of the other individuals who have designed with Johnson; however, the aim of this book is to probe the mind and art of Philip Johnson through his words and work. We made the selection of projects discussed in this book. Though this is only a sampling of Johnson's prodigious body of work, these projects are some of Johnson's own favorites, and according to him, make for some of the best stories.

The format of the book is a series of discussions that span Johnson's designs from 1942 to the present. These conversations not only detail the history and design of each project but also serve as a platform for Johnson to explain his views on architecture and how that approach has evolved over time. Johnson so infuses his work with his personality that it can be said they are one and the same. So Johnson's voice in combination with images is perhaps the best tool for sketching a portrait of Johnson's career.

We begin with Johnson's own residences in "The Architect at Home," in which he tells the story of building a house for himself while he was a graduate student at Harvard (1942) and explains the development (ongoing since 1949) of the buildings and grounds of the Glass House in New Canaan, Connecticut. In "A Pavilion and a Room," we look at two of his works for viewing art, the Museum of Pre-Columbian Art at Dumbarton Oaks (1963) and the Abby Aldrich Rockefeller Sculpture Garden at The Museum of Modern Art in New York (1953). Johnson's civic designs in "Building for City and State" are represented by the New York State Theater at Lincoln Center for the Performing Arts in New York (1964) and the Boston Public Library addition (1966-73).

Johnson has been described as more of a follower than an initiator, a perception he has done little to dispel. He often says, "I'm not a form giver like Mies," referring to the breakthrough works of modernism of Mies van der Rohe, Johnson's friend and mentor. But we do not fully agree with Johnson on this point. In "Breaking the Mold," he talks about designing a new form for a religious building in the Garden Grove Community Church, or Crystal Cathedral, as it is better known. We examine Johnson's claim to both fame and notoriety in the AT&T Building (1979-84), the work that made it acceptable once again to face a tall building in stone. The building also brought the term "postmodern" into the mainstream, though as early as the 1960s, with the lake pavilion in New Canaan and the museum at Dumbarton Oaks, his work was being described as postmodern, most notably by Robert Stern, whom Johnson credits with coining the term.

Today Johnson is known predominantly for his postmodern work in the 1970s and 1980s, when he designed high-end highrises for developers and corporate clients. He uses the chance to speak about these projects in "Patrons for Postmodernism" to clarify how important the client (or as Johnson is fond of saying, the patron) is to the end result of an architectural project. Many, but not all, of the buildings covered in this chapter are the product of Johnson's long-term professional relationship with Gerald D. Hines, one of the most high-profile developers in the United States, whose taste and talent, according to Johnson, made those buildings successful by measures of both business and art.

Some of Johnson's best work has combined architecture and landscape, arts that Johnson does not separate. About the designer of the gardens of Versailles he asks, "Wasn't Le Nôtre an architect?" This attitude is integral to Johnson's designs because it is the "processional element," or experience of moving through architecture, that drives his work. This effect is made clear when you walk from one pavilion to the next on his grounds in New Canaan or perhaps even more strongly in Johnson's Water Garden in Fort Worth, Texas (1970-75). Johnson has explained this concept in his writings, most notably in a 1965 article, "Whence and Whither: The Processional Element in Architecture." Johnson's interest in both landscape and placing objects within a natural environment is the focus of "Urbane Landscape," our conversation about his Fort Worth garden as well as the urban, yet tree-filled, campus of the University of St. Thomas in Houston, Texas (1957).

In "The Consistent Chameleon," Johnson-as-critic takes on Johnson-as-architect and his many changes in style in an open discussion of his design process, philosophical underpinnings, and views on architecture and other art forms. In our final talk with Johnson, "On the Boards," Johnson introduces the firm's latest projects, which include a new chapel in Houston, an office building in Berlin, large-scale commercial and residential projects in New York, and a new pavilion for his home in New Canaan. He speaks frankly about how current urban zoning restrictions and design guidelines discourage architectural innovation but, apparently undaunted, he goes on to announce boldly a new direction for architecture.

You might expect to find Philip Johnson surrounded by marble and gilt, reminiscent of his work at the AT&T Building or his other luxurious corporate temples of the 1980s. In truth, Philip Johnson has simpler tastes. His office is sparsely furnished: white walls, artwork from Jasper Johns, Michael Heizer, and Ed Ruscha and chairs by architects Frank Gehry and Robert Venturi. His desk is a round, black marble table upon which sit only a phone, his date book, and perhaps some yellow trace paper and an ample supply of freshly sharpened pencils. The office looks out on the East River and has a typical view of Manhattan's bizarre jumble of buildings.

Johnson is always beautifully dressed. He wears dark blue, sometimes gray, suits, with french-cuff shirts and handsome cuff links. He has worn his signature black, round-framed glasses, just like the architect Le Corbusier's, since the 1930s. Despite the formality of his appearance, his demeanor is relaxed. Perhaps this state of mind stems from the fact that Johnson has been at the center of things architectural in the United States for over 60 years, ever since he and Henry-Russell Hitchcock put together at The Museum of Modern Art the landmark 1932 show and book of modernism, *The International Style*.

But if you ask Philip Johnson about his place in history, he will respond modestly, "I'm not a big-name architect." This sort of unassuming comment is typical of Johnson in conversation, but it is undercut by his professional record. Johnson's contributions have earned him architecture's highest awards, the AIA Gold Medal and the Pritzker Prize. He has even graced the cover of *Time* magazine.

Still, many a critic has been willing to offer pointed assessments of Johnson, especially for his persistent subscription to formalism. The common claims are that Johnson isn't original, Johnson isn't consistent, Johnson isn't ideological. When asked why some critics fault his ever-changing style and clever quips, he responds with his typical irony: "It's just a dislike of chameleon-like publicity seekers." He then adds how unfortunate it is that the publicity his words attract, in fact, distracts people from his architecture. Does all of the negative criticism bother him? "It doesn't really matter." A smile. "Just spell the name right."

Such comments have often interfered with Johnson's work being as seriously considered as his quotes. (The media have always given him plenty of attention, yet there have been few books on his oeuvre other than those produced by Johnson or his colleagues.) His sense of humor can too easily be misinterpreted as derision, when in fact, on closer scrutiny, it is an aesthetic statement. Johnson loves a good visual pun, not to mention a verbal one. And while the critics may not be lining up to support all of Johnson's artistic efforts, the clients are. Johnson, at 88, is designing some of the largest projects in Manhattan: Times Square

Center (part of the 42nd Street redevelopment) for Park Tower Realty and Riverside South, a large-scale, mixed-use development for Donald Trump.

Johnson was born in 1906 in Cleveland, Ohio. His father, a wealthy lawyer, gave his young son some stock that turned out to be worth a small fortune. This meant Philip Johnson was fully funded for whatever he chose to do, not an insignificant fact in explaining how Johnson became involved with such interesting efforts as the nascent Museum of Modern Art and developing his own architectural practice. Johnson is fond of reminding students that one of the key elements to architecture is M-O-N-E-Y. While this bit of wisdom incenses some, it is hardly untrue. There are few professions that require more subsidy.

While an undergraduate at Harvard, Johnson studied the classics and philosophy. This training left an indelible mark on him.

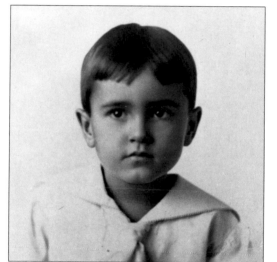

Johnson's humor, in fact, belies his quite philosophical nature. He admits to being greatly influenced by Nietzsche and Heraclitus. He calls Nietzsche a poet and he still reads him (in German). He heralds Heraclitus for that philosopher's embrace of the positive and inevitable aspects of change, which may contribute, in part, to Johnson's eager acceptance of new ideas and strong record of support for the work of young architects. On the other hand, he says he cannot accept Plato's insistence on absolute beauty and truth, which may explain, in part, why he has never settled on a solitary style.

Later, after graduating from Harvard in 1930, Johnson and fellow Harvardian and art historian Henry-Russell Hitchcock traveled throughout Europe documenting the "new" style of architecture that Johnson and Hitchcock would later label the International Style. When Johnson returned to the United States in 1932, he became the first director of the Department of Architecture and Design at The Museum of Modern Art. Johnson's link to The Museum of Modern Art is hardly random. The museum's first director, Alfred Barr, knew Johnson through Johnson's sister, Theodate, who had studied with Barr when he was a professor specializing in modern art at Wellesley in the 1920s. Johnson's connection with MoMA has continued ever since. Today as a Life Trustee of the museum, Johnson serves as honorary chairman of the Trustees' Committee on Architecture and Design as well as on several other committees. He has given the museum a substantial amount of art from his own collection.

Before returning to Harvard to study architecture formally, Johnson spent time in Germany in the 1930s. Johnson went to the Bauhaus in Dessau long before anyone in the United States was studying that establishment's new ideas about modern architecture and design. There he made contact with the architects who would later shape the form of postwar American cities, most notably, Walter Gropius and Ludwig Mies van der Rohe.

Johnson's own home, the Glass House, is modeled after Mies's Farnsworth House in Plano, Illinois. Even the furniture is by Mies. Johnson's rejection of Gropius and his allegiance to Mies separate him from other modernists. Mies van der Rohe is known for the artistry of his minimalist forms. His works are clear expressions of geometry and yet are refined and show a great attention to finishes. Mies was an artist; Johnson admires him for that.

Gropius, on the other hand, stressed how architecture was an expression of its own structure and function. Additionally, Gropius lauded modern architecture for its supposed ability to transform society. Johnson describes this as the "sociological side" of architecture and makes his own lack of faith in this attitude clear. For Johnson, architecture is a continuum not ruptured by modernism but comprising it.

Gropius joined Harvard's School of Architecture (now the Graduate School of Design) not long before Philip Johnson returned to Cambridge for his architectural training. Johnson insists that he was "not a Gropius man" while at Harvard. His inspiration there was Marcel Breuer, as well as Mies, despite his being in Chicago, where he headed the school of architecture at the Armour Institute (now Illinois Institute of Technology). Upon completing his degree in architecture in 1943, Johnson served in World War II. He then returned to New York and MoMA, where he produced many groundbreaking shows, including an exhibition of Mies van der Rohe's work in 1947. Johnson also wrote a book to accompany that show, the first on Mies. Most important, he finally began to practice architecture in earnest.

The greatest commission of Johnson's career has been his very own. His work at the Glass House has been the best leading indicator of the direction his style is going, from reminiscent International Style in the main glass pavilion (1949) – Johnson calls it a "1920s house" – to proto-postmodernism in his lake pavilion (1962), to hints of deconstructivism in his studio (1980), to his latest expressionistic work at the visitors pavilion that is now under construction. Oddly enough, there is no strong example of Johnson's postmodern opulence. There is, however, the playful "ghost house," a chain-link folly that is more an homage to Frank Gehry than to Johnson's own work of the 1980s.

This is not to say that Johnson has not had wonderful commissions. Though in the 1950s he mostly built homes for wealthy individuals, he soon became involved with large-scale civic commissions that included the master plans for New York University and Welfare (now Roosevelt) Island in New York City.

His experience with institutional commissions grew in the 1960s and 1970s. After he completed his sculpture garden for MoMA, museums became a Johnson specialty. He designed the Amon Carter Museum in Fort Worth, Texas (1961), the Sheldon Memorial Art Gallery in Lincoln, Nebraska (1963), the Museum for Pre-Columbian Art at Dumbarton Oaks, Washington, D.C., and the Art Gallery in Bielefeld, Germany (1968). He then moved on to libraries and civic buildings, creating, among others, the New York State Theater and the Boston Public Library addition.

Johnson loves a good patron, and he has worked with some of the best. His first exposure to the advantages of great patronage was when he was assisting Mies during the design and construction of the Seagram Building in New York (1956-59). There he had two patrons, Phyllis Lambert, now the director of the Canadian Centre for Architecture in Montreal, and her father, Samuel Bronfman, the head of Joseph E. Seagram and Sons. Shimon Peres had Johnson design a nuclear reactor, of all things, in Rehovot, Israel, in 1960. Nelson Rockefeller, one of Johnson's greatest supporters, commissioned the New York State Theater and the New York State Pavilion at the 1964 World's Fair, prompting Calvin Tomkins in a 1977 profile in the *New Yorker* to refer to Johnson as "architecte du gouverneur." In 1965, Johnson created a memorial to John F. Kennedy in Dallas for the Kennedy family.

Later in his career, Johnson would design for such diverse clients as Dr. Robert Schuller, the dynamic spiritual leader known for his "Hour of Power" television show, for whom Johnson created the Crystal Cathedral in Garden Grove, California (1977-80), and Gerald D. Hines, the developer of Pennzoil Place (1972-76) and many other elaborate office towers in the 1970s and 1980s. Recently, Johnson designed the new Museum of Television and Radio in New York for the late chairman of CBS, William Paley.

Defining Johnson's style is difficult. He has been more or less consistent in his treatment of proportion, order, and materials; however, he has espoused a wide spectrum of design ideas. You can usually spot a Johnson door – it tends to be a floor-to-ceiling rectangle that seems too tall and too thin to be quite right. That is just the way he wants it. Johnson is enamored of the effects created by the manipulation of scale, form, and proportion, and this obsession often results in quirky but beautiful forms, like the fat columns and low, domed ceilings at Dumbarton Oaks. He always uses beautiful materials – bronze, granite, and polished woods. As for workmanship, Henry-Russell Hitchcock pointed out that Johnson aspired to even more finely done brickwork than that of Mies himself.

But there is no single "style" that can be attached to Johnson's oeuvre because his architecture has changed so much over time. Rather, it is Johnson's mentality that has remained constant. That attitude can be summarized as a desire for elegance of materials and line, mixed with an ironic approach to forms. An example of this is Johnson's New York State Theater, with its spacious grand promenade, crowned in gold leaf and trimmed with marble and bronze but punctuated by playful, oversized sculpture by Elie Nadelman. Also, in the New York State Pavilion for the World's Fair of 1964, Johnson created an oval pavilion of columns that came out of his appreciation for the Italian baroque. The floor of the pavilion is an oversized Texaco road map of New York State.

Johnson's profound sense of humor, albeit one tempered by a sophisticated intellect, has occasionally irked critics. This has been especially true of his postmodern work in the 1980s, due to the familiar nature of the historic forms he used. Nonetheless, Johnson's humor is always present in his work and is at its most pointed in his work for himself.

This sensibility can also present itself in the form of irony, through the juxtaposition of forms or in an overall concept that Johnson calls "safe danger." A house made of glass is a fairly clear expression of this. Johnson injects this playful excitement into much of his work. Tempering this amusement with elegance is a trick at which Johnson excels.

Johnson reconciles these paradoxes in his landscapes as well as his buildings. His Fort Worth Water Garden is the most urban of natural settings. His mix of trees and controlled pools is structured by concrete steps; it's a park you can enjoy in good shoes. For the more adventurous, there are steps leading down into a chasm of rushing water that appear intimidating but are not really risky. Johnson finds these effects delightfully exciting.

Johnson claims he's a relativist. Aesthetically, this gives him the freedom to experiment with style without a firm attachment to any fixed design ideology. Johnson is a formalist, meaning he cares about what the building looks like in the end. Unlike architects schooled in the functionalist side of modernism, Johnson makes structure a means to a formalist end, not an aesthetic statement itself.

Some of Johnson's work, such as his lake pavilion in New Canaan and his out-of-scale lighting fixtures in International Place in Boston (1983-87), has been called pop. He rejects the label, saying pop was a very specific period in the 1960s and 1970s. No, he explains, his love of alteration of scale, ironic juxtaposition, and novel manipulation of forms comes out of a long tradition of architectural innovation.

He references Giulio Romano, the mannerist architect and painter of the sixteenth century who designed rooms that looked like they were being torn asunder by giants and courtyards that are ever so off-rhythm. Offering more historic precedents, he also cites Duchamp. Johnson, in fact, is a modern mannerist; he takes the familiar but then adjusts it, making it new. You only comprehend the manipulation if you know the original. For that, Johnson has been called an elitist. Ironically, he has also been taken to task by high-minded critics because much of his work is popular.

Johnson developed a fascination with architecture during his travels to Europe as a boy. He cites, in particular, the influence of the Acropolis in Greece and Chartres Cathedral in France. But Johnson is very eclectic in his selection of sources, which range from Sir John Soane, the eighteenth-century English architect, to Bertram Goodhue, the twentieth-century American known for his Nebraska State Capitol. Johnson is not capricious about his favorites. Asked to compare Bernini and Borromini, the two great architectural masters of the seventeenth century, Johnson quickly proclaims allegiance to Borromini, surely the more ironic and quick-witted of the two. Of course, never one to leave someone out, Johnson adds with a bright smile that he adores Bernini's brilliant colonnade at the entrance to Saint Peter's in Rome. Today he claims German expressionist Hermann Finsterlin and Americans Frank Gehry and Frank Stella as inspiration.

Perhaps less known is his love of the nineteenth-century classicist Karl Friedrich Schinkel, who also, according to Johnson, served as a model for Mies. Frequently, Johnson's style is described as European, probably because his buildings often incorporate the classical elements of balance and symmetry. Compare the centralized entrance in his facade for the New York State Theater with that of the Metropolitan Opera House or Avery Fisher Hall across the plaza at Lincoln Center. The differences are clear.

When we asked him where he would live if not in New York, he surprised us with the declaration: "When I turn 100 I think I will retire to Rome. The architecture there is so wonderful." Johnson the lover of things Italian? As it turns out, Johnson quotes Michelangelo as much as he does Schinkel. It is Michelangelo's design for the Capitoline Hill, or Campidoglio, in Rome that inspired Johnson's design for Lincoln Center's plaza, as well as for the ceiling in the New York State Theater. "If you like it, use it" seems to be his modus operandi, with little concern given to whether such a form is "appropriate." That may explain how the same Michelangelo-inspired form turned up on Johnson's carpet in the offices of Johnson/Burgee.

almost all the major architectural schools; to converse with him about architecture is to sit in on a master class. He knows his stuff, citing obscure built works as though everybody would know them. He loves a good conversation on his favorite subject, which he conducts with a scholar's grasp, a critic's take, and a practitioner's understanding. Johnson for decades has hosted intellectual gatherings in New Canaan, making the Glass House one of the great salons of twentieth-century architecture.

Johnson's interest in history was the driving force behind his excitement over postmodernism. As he describes it, it is a style well suited to his knowledge. Also, Johnson's love of historic architecture propelled him to fight for the preservation of great American architecture. Johnson has already arranged for the National Trust for Historic Preservation eventually to take over his Glass House. In the 1960s, when the preservation movement was just beginning to gain momentum, Johnson, along with Alfred Barr, publicly fought to save McKim, Mead & White's great Pennsylvania Station in New York. His interest in preservation is still strong despite the fact that he is one of new architecture's greatest allies and promoters.

Johnson is also interested in contextualism, despite his love of new directions. In his Museum of Television and Radio, Johnson was careful to work with the street line and, as he puts it, have the building be "a good citizen." Johnson loves cities and their complexities. He waxes eloquent on the wonder of the scale and layout of New York's SoHo district, adding that people animating the streets is what really makes that neighborhood so special.

Johnson differs from many contemporary practitioners and theorists in his belief in the art of architecture. His position has been consistent. As he reminds us when we discussed his and Hitchcock's book, as authors, their attitude was that modern architecture fascinated them for its outward appearance, its style. Given the influence of *The International Style*, both the book and the show, Johnson is often considered the great enthusiast of the modern style. Thus his departure from Miesian-inspired architecture, beginning in the 1950s in his redo of the guest house in New Canaan but made far more obvious in his "parrot-beaked" tops for the glass towers of Pennzoil Place, can appear to be a philosophical as well as an aesthetic about-face and has often been interpreted as a lack of conviction. Of course, the same change can also be seen as brave innovation. Johnson never shared the ideological view of functionalist modernism, so as he sees it, he is hardly a traitor to his beliefs. He loved the style of modernism but "grew bored with the box." Like any artist who tires of a style, he moves on to new things.

Johnson's interest in art is significant because he sees a relationship among all the arts, including architecture – "the mother of the arts." He admires paintings and has been collecting since he was a young man. Today he has an impressive collection of late–twentieth-century art, though most of it has been given to MoMA. His "Kunstbunker," as he amusingly refers to his painting gallery in New Canaan, is filled with works by Andy Warhol, Jasper Johns, Frank Stella, and others.

Johnson cites his sources like a historian. There is Mimar Sinan, the master of the Turkish baroque in Istanbul, in Dumbarton Oaks. There is Bertram Goodhue in the Transco Tower in Houston. There is even German expressionism creeping into the Crystal Cathedral. Perhaps most astonishingly, there is a bit of Frank Lloyd Wright in Johnson's current approach to skyscrapers. Of course, he may have identified these sources after he did the designs. Even Johnson concedes that. What matters is that he seems compelled to cite influences. Johnson tells of his frustration when a group of young architecture students on a visit to the Glass House would not own up to historic influences on their work. Their refusal to acknowledge the past's influence on the present is in fact the prevailing attitude in academic architecture.

In fact, Johnson is a historian. His studio (1980) at the Glass House is filled with books. There is a fireplace in the corner and a light-filled window through which he can see his Ghost House. Beneath a minaret-like cone sit his table, Frank Gehry chairs like those in his office, and piles of papers. There are manuscripts of books about him, papers by students, and drafts of essays and talks that he is working on. But the "monk's cell," as he calls it – it doesn't even have a bathroom – is really a container for the man and his books, which are all on architecture and arranged alphabetically. It is a working library.

Johnson's appreciation for the scholarship of architecture is perhaps obscured by his "public" persona but is essential to the way he works and designs. He has taught at Yale and lectured at

"Architecture is sculpture that is inhabited," Johnson says. But then he counters, "To think of architecture as sculpture is all wrong because of the question of scale." Despite the qualification, those are fighting words for many architects who maintain that architecture is not sculpture; it is an entirely different pursuit not to be confused with fashion and decorative arts. Johnson's attitude is far more tolerant. He accepts that there is a difference, but in formal and functional qualities, not philosophical ones.

Johnson's media image has been concocted out of various sound bites that he's unleashed over the years. Early on in our conversations with Johnson, for example, we asked him whether architecture was the oldest profession. Johnson laughed: "Oh no. It's the second-oldest profession." It's off-the-cuff answers like that that tend to get him into trouble. They also win him great aficionados who adore his wit. Indeed, he seemed genuinely surprised when we asked him about his fame (or infamy, depending on whom you ask) for having declared, "I am a whore and I am paid very well for building high-rise buildings," a remark made at an academic conference of architectural superstars in Charlottesville, Virginia. "That was just a casual remark," Johnson earnestly explains. "Why do people focus on that?"

Johnson speaks fondly of his native Ohio fields as some distant inspiration for his Glass House landscape. But if pressed, he emerges as a true New Yorker. When asked if he would rather not have to come to New York City for the work week, he seems astounded. "I'd be bored stiff if I were at the Glass House all week. Three days, that's it – back to where the action is."

New Canaan is his villa, his "refuge" from the city. Unlike the formidable Frank Lloyd Wright, who personally rejected the city and is considered all the more American for doing so, Johnson loves both, city and country. Is Johnson any less American for being an urbanite? Hardly. He represents the embodiment of the urbane American, sophisticated and part of society.

In *Philip Johnson: Architecture 1949-1965*, Johnson's first book of his own work, Henry-Russell Hitchcock wrote in his introduction: "Most architects at sixty are well past the mid-point of their careers, or used to be. But it is characteristic of twentieth-century longevity that leading architects . . . have continued productive into their seventies and eighties. So one may hope will Philip Johnson."

Hitchcock's hope has been easily fulfilled. Johnson, who started his building career as a man in his mid-thirties in 1942, is now best known for his work in the 1980s. It seems oddly appropriate that the elderly Johnson takes a briefcase of work home with him on the weekends. He loves to design and does not create a great division between his work and other aspects of his life.

The combination of a surprising use of scale and form, along with a knack for beautiful materials, gives Johnson's work a distinctive look that elicits strong reactions from observers. His interior for the Four Seasons restaurant is the appropriate setting for power lunches because the design itself – all that rich wood and polished surfaces – is so powerful. Is Johnson's architecture original? Sure. But with a strong base in tradition. Is it elegant? Al-

ways. You can make a joke with beautiful words or forms. Is it interesting? If most critics are willing to write strong words about the work, how could it not be?

Johnson, who loves clean simple lines and even clean simple sentences, is hardly a simple man. He is easily one of the most complex figures American architecture has ever seen. He is a clever but disarmingly straightforward writer, an able curator, an energetic enthusiast for the field, and foremost a very dedicated and serious architect. His works not only have made a mark on the cities where they are located but also have been models for many works by other architects. For someone whose casual quotes can easily appear in multiple dailies, he is surprisingly not someone who goes out of his way for attention. There is no publicist in the Johnson office. Imagine if there were.

It becomes clear after seeing all that Johnson has created and said that you have got to experience his architecture to really understand Philip Johnson. He can come up with some terrific verbal one liners, and has been accused of pulling off some architectural ones, which is either a compliment or a jab depending on whom you ask. But Johnson's best wit and intelligence is reserved for the visual object.

Hilary Lewis
Cambridge, Massachusetts, 1994

FRANK LLOYD WRIGHT WITH PHILIP JOHNSON

The Architect
at Home

Philip Johnson House, Ash Street
Cambridge, Massachusetts
1942

Philip Johnson House, Glass House
New Canaan, Connecticut
1949-present

At The Museum of Modern Art, Philip Johnson's role was critic and curator, not architect. He left his position as the first director of the Department of Architecture and Design to return to Harvard for the professional training he needed in order to pursue architecture as a career.

During his graduate studies in Cambridge, Johnson built his first home in 1942 on Ash Street. The house was a study in the "court-house," an idea he had absorbed from his mentor, Ludwig Mies van der Rohe. A court-house is an urban concept for containing a garden behind a tall wall, providing the homeowner with privacy and greenery.

Once inside the high fence that isolates the structure from the residential street of nineteenth-century homes, one comes upon an open view of a very private garden. The house is small, essentially one large room separated by partitions.

In Ash Street, Johnson was paying homage to Mies and trying out new ideas about prefabrication. The results were mixed. But the Ash Street house is perhaps most significant in that it presaged the Glass House in New Canaan, Connecticut that would become nearly synonymous with the name Philip Johnson. The Ash Street house still stands in one of Cambridge's toniest neighborhoods; it is now used as a study by the owner of the property next door.

What made you decide to go to architecture school?

Desperation. I wanted to do something, and I was a rich young fool wandering around in things I didn't know anything about. And, in fact, it got to the point where I wasn't doing anything at all. I thought, of all the silly things, why am I doing this? So I went to Harvard. That was the hardest thing I ever did, take that train to go up to Harvard.

Because you were leaving New York?

No, leaving my life. Leaving everything. Going out into the wilderness to seek my fortune. And I was grown up, it was too late to do that. I didn't know what to do. My life was in ruins. So I went out and had fun.

Did you enjoy your time in Cambridge?

Enormously. Just the opposite of what I thought. I thought I'd be no good and that I would be just laughed at by the kids – grandpa walking into the class.

How old were you?

In my thirties. Well, you'd look funny in a class of undergraduates, wouldn't you? But it didn't happen that way at all. Marcel Breuer was the best man. He was the only artist in the program.

Nor does it make a clean edge. But no, I thought of protecting the wall, from what I do not know. That was a mistake.

Did you learn any other lessons from building that house?

Yes, a lot of them. The wooden columns don't work too well. There were a lot of troubles. The way the bedroom wall comes out is not concluded. There should be a passage there, and I still don't know what I would have done. But that wasn't the right thing. On the other hand, the room itself is perfect. You can sit

That house, believe it or not, is prefabricated. This very tricky system worked all right, it just cost about twice what stud walls would have cost.

there in the snow in front of a roaring fire. It was a great idea, and it's still good.

The worst thing is the placing of the columns. I think I probably was gung ho about new technology, because of my training at Harvard. I had a marvelous time once it was built, because I used it as propaganda against Gropius. Once when he came to visit the house, the first time and the only time really, he walked smack into the wall and hurt his nose. It was bleeding.

Who was on the jury when you were doing your thesis at the Graduate School of Design?

There wasn't any jury. See, Dean Hudnut was a very casual, decent guy. I helped him find Mies and Gropius for Harvard. So we were friends before I ever went up there. One of the reasons I went to Harvard.

What did Gropius say when he saw the house? What was his response to it?

He didn't speak, and I didn't mention it. It was clear he was annoyed. The other thing was the passion – the typical Harvard thing – for new directions, new materials, new ways of building, and the prefab idea. That house, believe it or not, is prefabricated. This very tricky system worked all right, it just cost about twice what stud walls would have cost. That's what happens every time you prefab. Gropius started a prefabrication company that went bust the next year. The most expensive way you could possibly imagine building.

Let's not kid ourselves. The "mechanization takes command" point of view leads to madness. But Gropius never learned. Most people never learn because they're ideologists. I was. That frame of mind was catching, from the Gropius side of the Harvard educational system.

How many sets of plans did you go through before reaching a final design for the Ash Street house?

Well, I prefer not to remember the early designs. There were two different directions. One was a brick house. I was always crazy about bricks, through Mies, you see. And I loved the Tiffany House, Stanford White's, the Roman brick. Anyway, there was just one window, and it was awfully boring. I remember Henry-Russell Hitchcock saying to me, "That is very interesting material, Philip, but architecture?" I threw that out. I don't remember any other stages. And then the Mies influence was so strong, and his court-houses were so attractive, but nobody had ever built one. So I wasn't claiming any originality. It was a Mies idea. I wanted to see what a Mies court-house really looked like. I built one.

It's no longer used as a house; it's used as offices. Does it bother you that the house has been altered?

No way. It's almost an unusable house for more than one person. I left out everything, the way beginning architects always do. No storage, no attic, no basement. No place to put anything! Friends of mine bought it. So they later asked me, did I mind if they added a little room on it, in the court? I said I minded very much. So they sold the house. On the other hand, using it for a study is perfectly all right.

Did you ever use it as a studio?

No, no! Too small. I lived there. I had a come-in cook. In those days, of course, there were such things. And I lived very well. But

I left out everything, the way beginning architects always do. No storage, no attic, no basement. No place to put anything!

the other thing was to use the indoor-outdoor idea. It was wonderful for living outdoors because it was private. And that did work extremely well. In the winter, the furniture that was left there was deep in the snow.

Is the wall that surrounds the house original?

ASH STREET HOUSE, DINING ROOM

It hasn't been changed. The inventor of the system used to come from Washington State to supervise the installation. I thought I had really accomplished something, to build a prefabricated house.

It was a little expensive. In those days, of course, it seemed like nothing. I sold it for $24,000. For a year or so after I graduated, I had a friend living there. She enjoyed it very much. And

> # I thought I had really accomplished something, to build a prefabricated house. I sold it for $24,000.

then at the end of the war I realized I wasn't going to – you're right! I did build that house with thoughts of basing my life there. That's right, so I didn't sell it right away. I kept it through the war. But at the end of the war, I realized New York was where I wanted to be – and then I sold it.

Do you remember how much it cost to build the house?

I was much too clever to keep accounts. Never, never do that. I didn't keep records for the Glass House. But I spent more than a million on it.

A labor of love. You don't think about it.

You'd better not. You'd pale.

On Ash Street, did you have any special design for the garden that faced the bedroom areas?

Oh, yes. I'm really a landscape architect.

There was no water in the garden?

No. It never crossed my mind, thank goodness. Don't ever use water. Water does the damage. It finds ways of getting in the way.

You mentioned that you didn't keep records; you weren't thinking about the cost. Is a project where you yourself are the client more satisfying?

Far more, far more. Because if you make a mistake, you know it's your own and not because some client looked down your throat wrong. In fact, the one that was very much like building for myself was Mildred Bliss's Dumbarton Oaks. But of course, with all my own work for myself, if they're ugly, it's awful. Like that overhang. I'll never get over that.

Philip Johnson's residence in New Canaan, Connecticut, the Glass House, differs radically from the earlier house on Ash Street. It is located on a large piece of land – originally 5 acres, now over 40. The Glass House, as the entire property is known, has served not only as a country retreat for the architect, but also as a forum for architectural ideas. Recently, Philip Johnson bequeathed the property to the National Trust for Historic Preservation.

The first buildings to be completed on the property were the main pavilion, or Glass House (1949), and the brick guest house (1949, remodeled in 1953). Over the years, Johnson has added new pavilions that serve specific purposes: the lake pavilion (1962), the painting gallery (1965), the sculpture gallery (1970), the studio (1984), the Lincoln Kirstein Tower (1985), and the "ghost house" (1985). The latest addition is the visitors pavilion to be finished in 1994.

The Glass House is best seen in its entirety. It is made up of not only the main house but also an extended architectural study applied to landscape. The procession that takes a visitor from one pavilion to the next is one of the property's most remarkable features. A work in progress, the Glass House cannot be dated at 1949 – that is just its birth date.

When you approached the Glass House, were you still thinking about Ash Street, or was it essentially a new problem?

No, it was a new problem, but it is really both the same problem as well as a new one. The early design was a court solution. But actually, because of Mies's work with courts, it was natural to think that way. So Ash Street had its echoes. However, finally when I came to an isolated box, it was quite a break.

How close are your neighbors in New Canaan?

Out of eyesight. I used to be able to see one house, but I planted that out as soon as the trees came in. The Glass House is isolated. It's in its own garden just the way Ash Street is.

When you began your designs for New Canaan, were you thinking more about the overall site and the layout of the objects? Was the actual shape of the buildings secondary?

Well, I did buy the land because of the site and its narrow, rocky promontory that stuck out. I chose the site because of the famous Japanese idea: always put your house on a shelf, because the good spirits will be caught by the hill that's behind the house; the evil spirits will be unable to climb the hill below the house. Frank Lloyd Wright put it differently. He said never, never build on top of a hill.

The problem was, how do you approach the house without

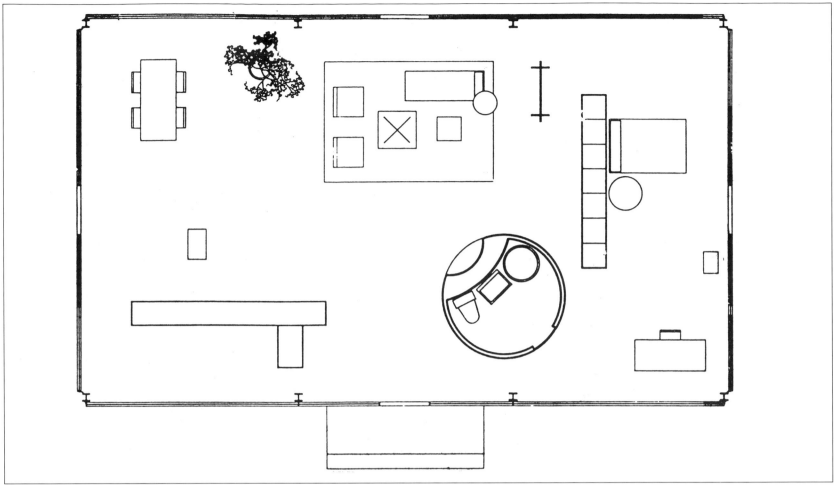

GLASS HOUSE, PLAN

looking down on it? For the first ten years, my driveway looked right down on the house. But later I bought the land next door and reconfigured the drive. So now it's fine, you come down and then you see the house. Those things are terribly, terribly important.

Then I had an early sketch with Syrian arches. That always fascinates scholars. I didn't realize that I was interested in arcuated buildings that early.

It was only a 5-acre plot. It's now 40. So it has developed over the 50 years that I've been working on it. In 1946 I bought the land, didn't I? So by 1996, that'll be 50 years.

Do you remember how many sketches or plans you went through before you reached your final scheme?

There were lots of early sketches before I got to the idea of keeping the Glass House out, and then putting the guest house back. I wanted to get it out all on the rocky promontory, of course,

but I found after a couple of years that the point was too small. It kept dropping off the edge. That was not good.

I had a U-shaped house at one time, with a semi-court, the fourth side being the drop. Then I had an early sketch with Syrian arches. That always fascinates scholars. I didn't realize that I was interested in arcuated buildings that early.

See, but that point was so rigid, and the trees were so big. I just couldn't take down the trees to change the whole, I couldn't change the landscape, because it was rigidly kept by the great old trees. How do you get a certain number of rooms on a point? By moving them back I was all right. Then I had the two sliding rectangles, although they were too far apart, really, to slip and slide. But I did it that way. Then you get a completely open pavilion, because there didn't have to be bathrooms or guest rooms or garbage bins. It really is a pavilion. But that came quite slowly.

Did you develop the idea of the views being at an angle when you decided to put the guest house off the point of the site?

Yes, everything is always at an angle. To me there isn't any front. It's pure classicism; it's pure Karl Friedrich Schinkel. I admired that kind of clarity of the axis – which I don't do so much of now. But I was classical. I didn't know that at the time, of course.

Really? When you were doing the original designs, didn't you think in the back of your mind, "This is a classical design"?

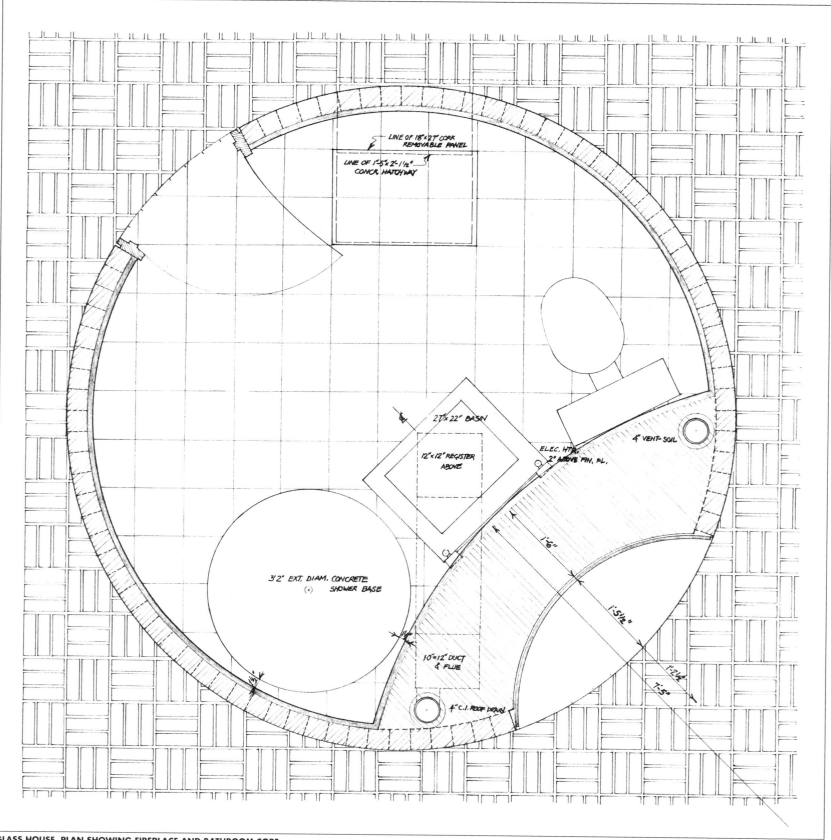

GLASS HOUSE, PLAN SHOWING FIREPLACE AND BATHROOM CORE

No, I was being Miesian. I thought the building was just a rip-off of Mies – of course it isn't. Mies's was a floating thing, a beautiful rhythm. Mine was the clunk that sits on the ground. But I wanted it to sit on the ground. Mine became almost like an American house, you step one step out and into nature. Mies's was like Le Corbusier – anti-nature. I was like Frank Lloyd Wright. Nature to Frank Lloyd Wright was fields, wetlands, and wild bushes.

Nature to Emerson also was kept nature. And my house is a house in the field. That comes from my upbringing in Ohio. I love fields, pastures. Pastures – I think it's because of the lines, or the walls in this case – provide an organizing grid that I've preserved in this landscape.

So there's a little latent Prairie School influence there.

Well not so latent since I was so anti-Wright at the time. But I wasn't really, you see, because I was brought up in the same kind of culture that he was. Except we didn't have the rolling valley he had. We were pretty flat and high.

We noticed one other seeming connection with Wright, and that was the off-center but still very massive brick chimney fireplace that flowed right into the brick floor.

Yes. That would drive Mies up the wall. For Mies that had to be differentiated from the base. Certainly not a masonry thing, certainly not a circle, and certainly not piercing the roof. In the Farnsworth House, you wouldn't know there was a fireplace or a bed within a hundred miles of it. That's probably why he couldn't stand the house. I wish he'd explained it to me. He refused to stay in the house.

The central chimney seems to be the heart of the house.

Yes, I think I've written of it that way – the anchor of the house, actually. It's absolutely important, because that's the hearth. See, Mies wouldn't have done that. Mies did use fireplaces, but the modern movement didn't – there were little things off in the corner like a Franklin stove, but never as the visual focus. But to me, backing up to a fire is just part of living in New England.

But did you recognize the fireplace as something Frank Lloyd Wright might have done at the time?

No, I didn't. To me, it was similar to my upbringing.

You also talked about how you had the imagery of a burned-out village as the idea behind your fireplace.

Yes, I regret having said that. Because the burned-out village was in the Second World War, and I was on the wrong side. So we don't talk about that anymore. My enemies do, of course. That's a part of my life that I'd rather forget.

But it was a horrifying sight. And yet, it's so symbolic, that you've got the hearth, the one thing that was left. And it was so beautiful. That's a horrible thing to say, but ruins are beautiful. You can't help it. Fascination with ruins, it's endless.

Then the Glass House is a glass-enclosed, modern interpretation of a ruin?

That's right. Without the glass casing, the house would float away. That feeling was in this village too; all that was left was the masonry. It gives you the complete anchor for the house. It's so anti-Miesian.

What is the shape of the fireplace in the Glass House? The opening itself, is it a square?

The opening itself is a rectangle because in a cylinder, you can't cut a curve. If you cut a curve it warps. Imagine cutting a circle in a cylinder. If you look from the side, it's distorted. So you cannot cut a curve in a curve. I see why you might say, wouldn't it be better, since it's a cylinder and it's curved to start with, to keep the curve. But no, you have to cut a cylinder with a slot. And that's what this fireplace is, a slot.

Did you ever consider lifting the house up on a platform?

In no way. The idea was to be connected with nature. But then again, I went completely classical with the parapet.

Even though the house is grounded to the plane, at night the floating roof gives the house an ethereal quality. What is your favorite time or view of the house?

Snow. Then you step into the house, and you stomp off the snow, and you put your backside up to the fireplace. We used to have snowy winters. But I'm afraid with global warming we'll

Trees are becoming the basic building material of the place. The framing of the view, the *repoussoir*. The accents are all done by trees.

never see them again. Then the snow comes down at night, and the building floats. If the snow comes down at an angle, then it's as if you're in an elevator going up that way. It isn't going straight up, because the snow never comes straight. You're being levitated, and that impressed me — really fantastic. It had very little to do with architecture.

Also with a glass house, from one side of the house you see the moon rise, while from the other side you see the sun, both at the same time.

Do you think of the house as a pavilion?

Oh, yes. I think of it, again from my youth, as the village bandstand. In the Labor Day celebration my hometown had, we loved it. The bands would come in and play, in just an open pavilion. But you see, the band was slightly raised above the crowd. But the place was open and you could see in all directions into the woods, over the heads of the people.

That's what I have. It's a pavilion that watches over nature, and looks at the stone walls and the trees. Trees are becoming the basic building material of the place. The framing of the view, the

GLASS HOUSE, INTERIOR WITH STUDIO IN THE DISTANCE

I covered the walls with Fortuny fabric that is pink – but you'd never think of it that way – with some gold and silver. The fabric is not blank like a modern one; it has a little pattern.

Which of your guests seemed to appreciate the property the most?

Well, Mary Callery was my close friend – a sculptor. She was a bad sculptor, but a wonderful woman, and Mies's girlfriend at that time. She appreciated what was happening, and she spent the first night with me up there, New Year's Eve, 1949.

Finally, she wouldn't stay there anymore, because I didn't have a bed light. Which I couldn't have. It would spoil the effect. Effect before everything.

Have you ever had guests admit to you that while they're very happy to stay in the brick house, they really would prefer to stay in the Glass House?

One couple I did let stay in the Glass House. I went and slept in the brick house. They were my clients at the time. That was in the 1950s. I've never let anybody else. I stopped having guests, they're nuisances.

What is your favorite spot in the whole complex?

I just sit outside the house – a sitting place under a tree. It faces the slope down, and you can turn and look up. Then you look over and see the sculpture gallery and painting gallery.

What were you thinking about visually when you were designing the picture gallery?

I wanted it to look just like a naturalistic mound. I did show the edge of the roof, the parapet, to mark it as a building and not just a God-made hill. It became part of the landscape rather than making a statement as a building. It's also true that I didn't want any windows. I was in the school of installation work at that time with Alfred Barr, which said you shouldn't have daylight in a museum because the sun's bound to get in and ruin things. With windows you don't get to control the amount of light on your pictures. So being of that school – of which I no longer am – I decided to keep the light out of that gallery.

The whole design of an underground museum was interesting. I get museum fatigue very early on in a museum. Fifteen minutes is about my speed. For instance, the best museum in the world to me is that little chapel that is so hard to get to in San Sepulchro. It's got the greatest picture in the world, a Piero della Francesca. I like seeing only one picture at a time. When I saw that I said "ah-ha." And then of course when I was designing the gallery, I thought of how the Japanese never show more than one *takonoma* at one time.

So I asked myself, how do you combine those things? How do you reduce the number of pictures you're looking at so that the amount you can grasp is in a single field? And how can that be done? And I developed this very beautiful system. It should've been used by other people since. But I now realize why that hasn't happened, but that's another point. I arranged them on "postcard rack" walls that twirl around. And I put three of these racks, of different sizes, in three different circles in the room, as it were. So I can get big pictures on the big walls that turn around, and the same for the small pictures. The result is that I can see two, four, or six pictures – two on each wall. Six pictures is a fine number. The room is 40 feet square. And you do get to see the big pictures, the middle-size pictures, and the small pictures at the same time.

The reason why museums can't use this system is control. Because the public can get behind the racks, and God knows, they can slash the paintings or something. It is an idea that everybody admires, but nobody can do. But it works wonderfully for looking at pictures.

Are you still as pleased today with the pavilion by the lake as you were when you first produced it?

Oh, more so! I just cleaned it up. After 30 years it looked pretty bedraggled. For the Trust I did fix it up. It's the old feeling I have, that everybody has, of a tree house or a doll's house. I had to do something. A blank American landscape, it's the dullest thing in the world.

The little pavilion, of course, had a lot more to it than just being a folly or a gazebo for a house in the English manner. The folly I used as an experiment. One thing I wanted to test was the use of pre cast concrete. The forms were made in Holland. The pre-castings were put up in one night. I remember staying awake most of the night listening to them because I got so mad because it was so late. But anyhow, they built it in one night. And I thought that was a great accomplishment. It should have been cheaper than regular construction. In fact, it cost two or three times more, but that's all right. We found out that we could build in precast, which is a very difficult material.

Then I also had an aesthetic problem, which was more interesting to solve. The flattened arches, of course, I stole from the redo of the guest house above. That's why I used the same flattened arch. The toed-in base I got from Robert Delaunay from his pictures of Saint Severin. I just like it, that's all. I can't give you a reason why an arch has to be toed-in at the base. It doesn't have to be. But I thought it looked right here.

The most important problem I had was in a portico court. When you go around the corners and you're arcuating each corner, how do you enter the court? When you have two arches leaning on one corner – the terrible problem from the Renaissance – what do you do about that corner arch? One poor little arch, at one corner, holding two great arches. The problem wasn't solved until Laurana did the design for the ducal palace in Urbino.

In his courtyard in Urbino, what did he do? He added an extra column. And since then you've never had any trouble at all with

the arches coming down on the corner. Well, I wanted to design an arch that would look two ways. Instead of an arched portico, just making rhythms, I wanted to be able to turn a rhythm at 90 degrees. So I invented this arch that has a way of starting a column, either on the side or across from it. I was very proud of myself for solving the great Laurana question from the Renaissance. But all those things take endless time to solve. And everything you do, everything I've done at least at my place, has been that sort of double experiment.

So you experiment first on your own property before you experiment on someone else's project?

That's what I like to do.

I separated the lake pavilion out from the mainland, so it's really hard to reach. It's a big step up across the water. I can no longer do it, by the way. It's very hard. If you're very tall and young, you can do it. But that's important. It's part of the necessity of struggle

It's exactly the same as a kid building, or having his father build, a tree house. You pull the rope in after you and it's yours.

for getting to any beautiful object. In getting to an island, you feel separated from the mainland, and therefore on your own. That, incidentally, has sexual overtones that I don't understand, because I don't read my Freud very well. But it is a feeling of excitement, like being on a ship when you first cast off from land.

It would be very helpful if you could explain your term, "full scale, false scale," which you have used in describing the pavilion.

In planning it I had a lot of fun. I reduced the scale of the pavilion for several reasons. If you come into a room that's the wrong scale – like the dwarves' quarters in Mantua – that gives you a wonderful feeling of power. Power, being also sex, is a very wonderful feeling. So I said, let's make this pavilion small. I did it at about half scale. So when you walk in, you hit the ceiling if you're a tall person. You can just get in if you are short. But tall people have to duck. That feeling of being powerful and big is a marvelous feeling. I still reduce myself to the proper scale when I am in the pavilion. I can make myself small by imagining – you can do that, you know. If you sit down and think hard, you can think of the right scale. To me it becomes full scale then.

I also planned the circulation through the rooms. There are about five little rooms. I say "rooms" in quotes, because they're all just arches dividing the space. Of course, the routes from room to room became quite clear. You can walk from this room to this

room, but you can't go from that room to that room, because you'd have to step across the water. And of course that's much too "far" if you're in the proper mood. You can't do that. You can't go around that corner and step diagonally across, because it's just too *far*, if you were that *small*. Or rather if the pavilion were that *big*, see? And so I don't let people make that step, because I want them to try to make themselves feel small the way I can. And they can't all do that. Then I named the rooms: the dressing room, the library, the living room, and the bedroom.

How did you decide which was which?

It's very easy when you're there. For example, the dressing room is obvious, because in it you can't be seen from the main house. There's the living room, because it's two units put together. It becomes clear when you are in the "house."

Did you name the rooms afterward or during the original design?

Oh, no, afterward. That's the whole point, the whole experience, of a playhouse. That's what this is of course, a playhouse. It's exactly the same as a kid building, or having his father build, a tree house. You pull the rope in after you and it's yours. Or a dollhouse for a girl. She thinks right away back to the scale of the dolls that are in that little house. I do in the pavilion. You can get into the scale of it, and that gives you quite a kick. I don't know why. Alice in Wonderland. The change in scale forces you into whatever the scale is.

That's what the people at Disney understand very, very well. People love a change of scale. It's too big, it's too small, it's marvelous.

Indeed. There are so many elements that come into that pavilion: the change of scale, the experiment with materials, the planning of the rooms. The planning of the rooms comes from Mondrian. The arches are from Delaunay's Saint Severin. The corners are from Laurana. As for the change in scale, since it was built before I went to Disneyland, I did not get it from there. But it certainly was part of the same thinking. But I did get that from the dwarves' quarters in Mantua, which excited me so when I saw them.

I think that architecture is so much more than thinking about shape or anything. It's the whole cultural side that you roll up into the design. The architect is expressing his whole cultural background and experience in a building. And so it isn't just the placing of a window. Each building is the expression of a cultural background of a whole lifetime. I had more than my usual share in that building because I didn't have a function for it. I did not have those three impediments to architecture: clients, function, and money. It wasn't expensive. So I'd gotten rid of all three of those things in one stroke. The pavilion is the one clearest expression of architecture on the whole place. I don't say it's the best. I say it is the clearest expression of what architecture is for.

Did it bother you when the critics responded negatively to the lake pavilion? Some said that the folly was not architecture.

In the first place, they had never seen any postmodern work. But the most acid critic was my best critic, Kenneth Frampton, who wrote by far the most significant article on the subject. He asked how a man could imagine something as brilliant as the Glass House and yet do something so ordinary and common as the pavilion. But of course, I don't mind that. Well, I minded, naturally, but only slightly. But what I claim is nevertheless right. Good or bad, small or big, that is the purest time that I ever had in my life to do architecture. Everything else is tainted with the three problems: clients, function, and money. Here I had none of the three.

They die hard, these ideas one has about materials. But some things worked. The idea of the tree house – back to a childhood dream world – works very well.

In your 1950 writings on the compound, you talk about how the layout is similar to the Acropolis.

Well, that was when it was a very much smaller grouping. It ceased to be an Acropolis when I bought all the acreage. Then it became a bit like English landscape.

Are you more attracted to English landscape than to, for example, French landscape?

Oh my, yes. As much as I admire Le Nôtre, he was too rigid. I used to travel around England in the summer, looking at the estates and the incredible gardens.

Do you see a contradiction in a modernist construction that is essentially Miesian, like the Glass House, that turns out to be a picturesque landscape?

That's what architecture is as it develops – it transforms into different things. Oh, no, but a construction like the Glass House isn't English landscape; it's all laid out on New England fields. Seventeenth-century New England. The walls are just American stone walls. People come from Europe and say, "Oh heck, where did you get these stone walls?" Well, hell, those stone walls were there long before I came.

Tell us about what you call the "anti-deer house."

I found an old basement deep in the woods, covered in vines. It was the foundation of a cow barn. It must have been in service around 1900, because there was a cement floor. There were a lot of little granaries around. This foundation was in the woods, but it isn't any longer because I've been cutting so drastically. Now you see it perfectly well. I loved those ruins and kept them and built on top of them. It's a little pavilion – a chain link fence thing.

GHOST HOUSE

I built it the way a child designs a house, but I left the gable off. It's open, you can get through and all around. You can walk in. But it keeps the deer out and it keeps the lilies inside. Preserved. The great enemy in our part of the country are the deer. The Bambi lovers won't let me shoot them. But they're kept out, and I still get my sense of the old cow barn. It's just another little object in the landscape. Sometimes we call it the "ghost house."

If you built additional items for New Canaan, would they be pavilions of that type?

Always a pavilion. I built another one, which is now the library, the studio. I spend weekends there. It's a 15-by-15-foot room, a monk's cell, supposedly. There is one window where I can watch the rain or nature or leaves falling off, but be totally enclosed. People think the studio's Islamic, because in one corner is a truncated cone, like a dome, which is really a light source, and in the other corner a chimney that looks like a minaret. Wonderful nondirectional light. There is one window looking out toward the little anti-deer house.

Is that connected by any path?

No, I don't like paths. No paths. I've been having trouble with the National Trust. See, old ladies have to have paths. Well, they don't have to visit the studio.

43

Before you built the studio, where did you work?

I worked all over the place in the Glass House, which is very unsatisfactory to work in. Too many distractions. Squirrels! Birds! Reflections don't bother me, but the lack of containment does. The studio – I got the idea from Mexico – is a little monastery room. This is a wonderful little place to get away, build a fire, but no water, no toilets, no nothing. I didn't want any distractions. It is mostly filled with books.

Do you find that distractions can be a problem in the Glass House in general?

If you feel like getting to work right away, there are no distractions – because of the fireplace. You don't feel any distraction if you're out on a camping trip and you're roasting wieners. It doesn't cross your mind, because there's a focused sense. It's a permanent camp – the Glass House is a permanent camping trip protected from weather.

Tell us about the tower.

I built a tower above the pavilion down beyond at the lake. It's beautiful. It is a staircase that goes to nowhere, and it's very, very steep. I used concrete blocks, so the steps are all very, very high. The risers and the treads are also eight inches. Very awkward. And of course, you're up in the air with no support, no nothing. Very narrow, no railings!

The little old ladies from the National Trust are not going to be very happy.

The tower is dedicated to Lincoln Kirstein, the poet. I can go up, but Lincoln Kirstein himself has never been up. Some people are acrophobic, most people. I love that sense of a perfectly safe danger. For instance, my bridge is 3-inch steel that spans 30 feet, and it's very narrow, 4-feet wide. So old ladies are going to think, "Oh, I can't cross over that."

At what point did you decide that you wanted a separate sculpture gallery? You already had the painting gallery.

That's a very, very sharp question, much sharper than you know. I had no intention of building another building then. But I had some shapes in mind that I wanted to make real. It was perfectly clear to me that I'd made a perfectly horrifying mistake in the painting gallery. Where would you put sculpture when the great postcard racks start turning? You'd have to get out of the way. Therefore you'd have to move the sculpture over to another place while you turn the rack. So it didn't work. I had to build another building because I had to show sculpture, of course. And besides, the real reason is, as always, I wanted to build another building. Then I realized that the building I wanted to build was a staircase. I separate my buildings into "inside" and "outside" buildings. The sculpture gallery is a pure inside building, as is the painting gallery.

In the sense that it's most important to see these from the inside, the outside is not the issue?

Yes, it's not an issue, nor is it particularly attractive, all of these angles screaming out at you.

But doesn't that bother you? You see it from the outside all the time since you live right there.

It bothers me only marginally. Because if I'd let it bother me, I'd have to build a skin for it, or design an outside for it. Do you suppose that both those galleries not having any outsides tells you something about either my ability as an architect, or my concentration in architecture at that point? I think the latter, because I can't believe that I'm not interested in outsides of buildings. At that point I was interested in interiors. And I got fascinated by great staircases by way of the Renaissance and the baroque, especially the baroque. But also with any experience where you go up and down, like the great stairway in China that I've only seen in pictures. That goes way, way up the side of a mountain. A terrific experience, just the fact of those lines being there. Or the great staircase where you go up on your knees in Rome. Then, of course, I was influenced by the Greek islands. There, every street is a staircase to somewhere.

It has the feel of a Mediterranean village.

Of course, it's very Greek island in its feeling. The main thing was a staircase going around an open atrium, which is not such an unusual thing. But I was so tired of square atria, or courts, I couldn't stand it. So how do I break that? So I broke it in a rather curious way. I took the square, and I took the roof around it and put it on 45 degrees. Then I took some of the walls and used that

I separate my buildings into "inside" and "outside" buildings. The sculpture gallery is a pure inside building.

grid from the roof and another set of walls from the floor. Which meant that I could choose between which grid I was using when I designed the walls. This is a central court with five bays. It was a pentagon when I got through with it. By using the proper angles, I had five bays off five sides. And those five bays became the five galleries for sculpture.

And having those five separate sculpture galleries again, in turn, came from my feeling about sculpture galleries in general, especially those in The Museum of Modern Art. There you look at a sculpture, but your peripheral vision is occupied with all the rest of the sculpture in the room. You cannot see sculpture with another sculpture behind it. Too much competition. So I made these bays very shallow so that no one sculpture is behind another sculpture. And each bay was a different height. They all went

I think someone should commission me to do a house on the principles of the Greek village and the climbing of hills. I'd build one in the country.

up to the same roof, but the bays were higher as you went down the steps.

Another part of my reasoning was my feeling for the processional. The processional in this pentagon is delicious. You're going down and down, and when you're through, you feel like the famous dog that sniffs his way all the way around in a circle until he curls up and lies down in the proper part of the circle. When you get to the bottom, you feel, "Now I'm where I'm supposed to be. I've done it, I can go to sleep." That is all very, very important in architecture, how you feel as you go by these various things on the different levels, each with its own little sculpture show. I broke that down so you remember the different sculptures that you liked, but that's all.

The whole thing is really one of my most successful rooms. In fact, I liked it so much that I thought I would put all the sculpture down in the glass house and make the gallery into a house. It would be such fun, you see. The lowest room would be the pool, the inside pool. The middle section at the bottom of the stairs is your entrance hall. The first gallery up, the first bay up, would become the living room where you sit and look down at the entrance hall while you're enclosed in one of the bays. The lowest part under the entrance would be the bed quarters. But that would be air-conditioned and sealed off, not really part of the composition. And the kitchen would be where you come in, on the second level from the top. It was all very simple, I would have had a lot of fun doing it.

Would there have been enough room to put all the sculptures in the Glass House?

No, it would have been all wrong for the sculptures. That's why I wasn't too serious about the change. I think someone should commission me to do a house on the principles of the Greek village and the climbing of hills. I'd build one in the country. It would be great.

How many more buildings do you envision for the compound?

I've got one more to go, the visitors pavilion. It's for the people that come and pay their good money. That building is going to be so entirely different that it will surprise everybody – they will leave either with a sour note or an interesting note. It's done in my latest style, all in curves and anti-geometric shapes, as if it were a piece of enormous sculpture. It's about 20-feet high, but it's an infinitesimal building, only about a thousand square feet. It's going to be several colors and built using a new technique.

But as you know, with all the buildings on the place, I've always experimented both with the structure as well as with the form. And so this time I experimented with a new kind of wall. My engineer, Ysrael Seinuk, introduced me to this way of building.

It's a way of spraying concrete, like when you build a swimming pool. It's like gunite, but the core on which you spray this stuff is a bendable and movable cage of metal. If I don't like a curve when it gets up there in real life, I can change it. The bulges and the warp of the walls can be altered.

You see, with most materials you can't warp it like you can a piece of clay or bronze. But with this I can actually change the form while I'm building it. You can see whether the sloping walls and the sharp lines and the rises of the points of the building will be good or bad. So this is a brand new world we're stepping into and that will be my last building on the place.

Is there a new term for this technology?

Oh, no. It's a patented system invented, I think Ysrael told me, in Italy. It's been used in Florida and Israel for cheap housing, because it's the cheapest method of building and can be put up by

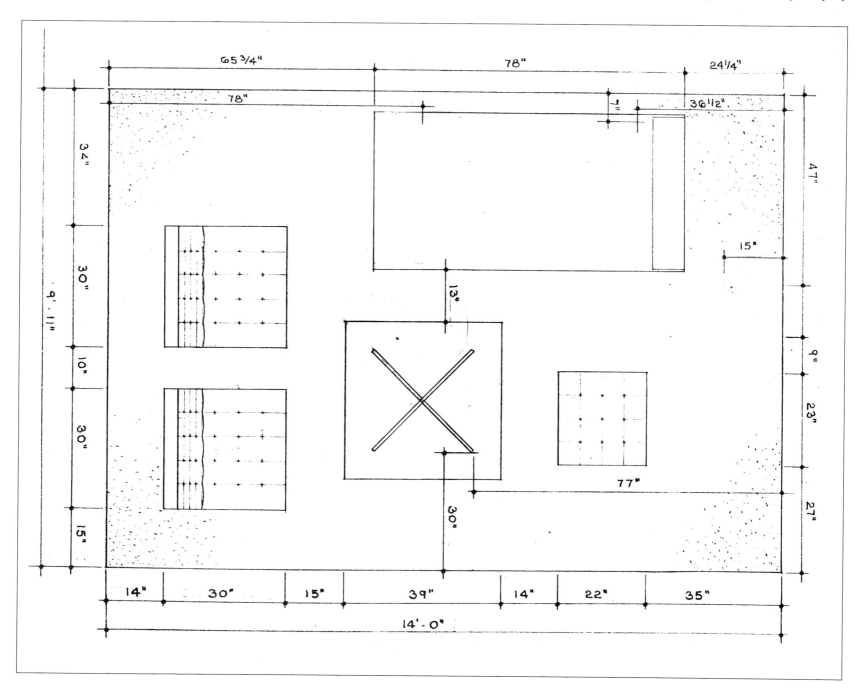

GLASS HOUSE, PLAN SHOWING PRECISE FURNITURE PLACEMENT

VISITORS PAVILION, RENDERING

unskilled labor. The floor, the roof, the covering of the roof, the walls, and the partitions are all made of the same material. It's got insulation in it.

Is your attraction to this technology due to its malleability?

Malleability, that's the word I've been looking for. It's a malleable way of building walls and roofs. And because the walls and roofs are all the same material, the roof is still the same color as the wall, like a piece of sculpture. As a matter of fact, it's going to be fun.

Is there a name for this phase of yours that comes out of this building technique?

No. But it has been in the back of our minds. "Our" minds, because it's something that Peter Eisenman and Frank Gehry, and the painter-sculptor Frank Stella are all working on. The nearest analogy is the work of an unknown German architect named Finsterlin, who's an exact contemporary of Mies van der Rohe. But he never got over the 1920s, or really the late teens, of this century. That was when expressionism was the vogue all over Germany. But it didn't actually spread to any other country. It was a fantastic time, and Finsterlin was the most extreme of expressionism's proponents.

But the man who made expressionism in architecture famous and actually carried out a building in it was Erich Mendelsohn, who deserves a great deal of credit for developing the style. But he was very disappointed because he had to build his Einstein Tower out of brick and cover it with stucco. That was the only way it could be built. So he gave the style up and went as everyone else did to modern architecture. But nowadays since things are becoming possible through new technology, why not experiment? I'm just delighted to play around with new technology.

There are some critics who would say, well, that's fine for sculpture, but architecture still has to provide a solution to a problem. What's your response to that?

I think they have something, those critics. Because the catch is, how do you put a window in it? You will notice there are no windows in the models I have made. In my new pavilion, there is a window in it. I'll show you how we do it, but I'm not sure it's right. But to put in a lot of windows! That's a challenge.

The man who gave you the Glass House now gives you a house without windows.

See? That's a good reason to do no windows in this building.

How would you build your own residence on that site today if there were no Glass House?

Oh, I don't know, how can I? It took me 50 years to build this. I'll start over, thank you. It would probably be what I have in my mind now, anti-geometric shapes. It would have to be very strange, no regular verticals: curves, saddle shapes, slopes. You see with the new materials – here I go again – you can do these things. Built in color. That is what I am doing now.

I think my next building will be a tomb, don't you think? I've been thinking about it for many years, but I don't feel like a tomb right now. The nearer one gets to it, the less one thinks about it.

I designed a tomb for a client in Germany. But the town raised such a stink. They're socialists there, and this man was very wealthy. But they screamed and yelled that he was spending money on it and moving tombs around. We had to build a new setting. He gave it up.

That would be interesting though. Like Louis Sullivan's Getty Tomb. It's so beautiful.

Sullivan was more a decorator, detailer than an architect.

Some critics are troubled by the Glass House because you can see right into it. They interpret it as a form of exhibitionism.

Yes, needless to say a great number of them have said that. In fact, they went so far as publishing in a magazine, "People that live in glass houses should ball in the basement." But I don't have a basement, so I don't ball in the basement. But much more important than exhibitionism is the interface of architecture and the desire for all kinds of sexual experiments. Whether you want to close yourself in is Freudian in one way, but exposing yourself is Freudian in another way.

As a good Puritan Unitarian, it did not come to mind, but there are other ways of having it come to mind. I mean the idea of a glass house, where somebody just might be looking – naturally, you don't want them to be looking. But what about it? That little edge of danger in being caught. Sometimes a little kid masturbates because he wants to get caught. And the whole question of safe danger in my plans – whether the bridge is a little bit narrow and gets you a little frightened – is that sexual or not? Probably. Certainly sex and designing are intimately connected. But I don't think there's been enough research yet, if ever, to connect the two definitely.

But there's no question in my case. It's like my desire for an island. Just why should an island be sexy? Why is a tree house sexy? They are. And my sense of an island is, I don't know, a sense of the forbidden. I do what I want to do. But much more work should be done on that. It's a fascinating subject.

The more we think about the Glass House, the more the entire composition seems to be essentially a villa. There's no way you can separate the house from the land; it's an integral composition.

It's always a landscape. That's what took me so long, because the piece of land I had was not large enough for a house. It's a promontory of a certain size. You couldn't change it because of the 100-year-old oak tree. So I was stuck with a promontory sticking out from a hill. Well, in the first place you never can see the promontory in any photographs, or in any drawing, so it doesn't exist to most people. But you're right, you're absolutely right. And that's what Jeffrey Kipnis points out in the Glass House book: that it's really a 40-year architectural design. It's a continuing process. The house and that promontory were the first part I landscaped. But since then, I've bought all this land and I keep extending it outward, like an English landscape.

Well, sure, it's like an American house: the indoor-outdoor thing. It wasn't formalist. It was a place where you could live and easily get around in the landscape. And the Miesian one [the Farnsworth House] is a cold, abstract object that you climb a series of stairs and turns to reach. It's like being in a temple with the proper steps.

Do you think of it as your primary or secondary residence?

It's the primary one. My apartment in New York is a pied-à-terre. I would be bored stiff at the Glass House all week. Three days, that's it – get back to where the action is. But I find as I grow older, I need more time to rest.

Are there any parts of the Glass House that you look back on and say, "I wish I'd done that differently?"

It's all right, wonderful. I didn't make the same mistakes I did in Ash Street.

You learned from Ash Street.

Learning from Ash Street. I'm very grateful to the dean for giving me my degree – I was drafted that day.

A Pavilion and a Room

Museum for Pre-Columbian Art, Dumbarton Oaks
Washington, D.C.
1963

Abby Aldrich Rockefeller Sculpture Garden
The Museum of Modern Art
New York, New York
1953

When Mildred Bliss decided to add a gallery to her estate, Dumbarton Oaks, in Georgetown, she turned to Philip Johnson. Mrs. Bliss helped Johnson develop the jewelbox-like pavilion that is just barely attached to the main building. The museum houses a collection of pre-Columbian art assembled by Mrs. Bliss's husband, Robert Woods Bliss. The museum, house, and the property's extensive gardens were donated to Harvard in 1940 by the Bliss family and are now a center for Byzantine and Landscape studies.

Johnson spared no expense using teak, marble, and glass to create a sumptuous setting for the assemblage of small objects. Supremely elegant, the pavilion has that Johnsonian quality of being slightly the wrong scale. The roof is low, the columns so large that they are more objects than supports. The domes amplify the faintest sound to a broadcast-like boom.

To create this pavilion, Johnson drew on his knowledge of Turkish and Islamic architecture and its use of the floating dome of the Madrasa, or school. Nine interconnected domes focus on a central fountain. Completed in 1963, the pavilion is both Islamic and classical in form. And because of this radical combination, none other than Robert A.M. Stern described the pavilion as "postmodern" almost 30 years ago.

This is a fabulous pavilion. Were you more concerned about what the museum felt like on the interior than on the exterior?

It is only an interior.

The exterior is just not an issue?

No, the whole trick here is an interior building surrounded tightly with woods. I didn't know enough about horticulture in those days to realize that the trees won't grow up tight to a glass wall; they tend towards the sun, so there is a little light around it. It's meant to be in a forest like that. But you never get just what you want.

The idea I was after was woods enclosed, because the worst thing in a museum is glass. The last thing you want is for your eyes to keep wandering away from the art. That's why I like the greenery to grow as close to the building as you can possibly persuade it to grow.

Did you choose the plants? The museum seems to be enclosed on two sides by very dense holly trees.

The holly was chosen because I needed the density there against the street.

And you knew that the trees would fill in?

Yes, well, I had my partner, Mrs. Bliss. I thought it should be the firm of Johnson and Bliss. She did a good deal of the work. She knew what would grow, and there were gardeners, so there was no trouble getting help. That was one of those lucky things that happened. Very few times you get a perfect client with a perfect program with all the money in the world. There's one or two – Mies and the Tugendhat House, for example.

Yes, well, I had my partner, Mrs. Bliss. Very few times you get a perfect client with a perfect program with all the money in the world.

But this was the most interesting job I ever had; it was a joyous pleasure to work. I mean, I had none of those troubles I had with other buildings of a practical nature, because everything was taken care of. I didn't know who the contractor was. I said, "Do this, do that," the way an architect was supposed to do in previous centuries. Now it's all paperwork.

You had a "lady patron bountiful" to help you.

"Lady patron bountiful" with an eye; that is a combination. Oh, the most interesting part of the job was when we mocked up one of these cylinders, in the concert room. We took everything out. Full-size mock-up with everything – all the details. I remember the bronze, I changed the height and the depth of those little ridges on that model, and Mrs. Bliss was, of course, fascinated because she couldn't imagine as I could what it would look like. This gave her an accurate picture of what one of the cylinders would look like. That's the way to do architecture. Then you don't have to tear it apart afterwards.

Did she have any input at all in the design?

Oh, my, yes. But it's hard to remember exactly how. I think she helped with the flooring. She picked the marble. I had to get samples and samples for her to look at. She loved the idea of the fountain and the edge slate.
The fountain is from Sir Edwin Lutyens. The slate was fractured beautifully and in a wedge shape that mimics the floor.

The materials you used here, such as the wedges of teak, are very luxurious, yet elegantly restrained. The dark green polished marble forms a precise sort of circular plinth around the bottom. What made you decide on the level of finish, and was it Mrs. Bliss in particular who chose those finishes?

No, no, I did. But she was very much in on all of the discussions. Since my memory is a self-serving tool, it's possible that she had even more input. I think she could have changed things from oak to teak or something like that.

How did you arrive at the wedge and circular motif that goes through the building?

That's very simple. If you have a circle, that's what you get.

The way that you put the forms together appears to be Byzantine or Islamic. Was this a form that you wanted to use in general, or was it because of the collection that you felt this was appropriate?

No, it had nothing to do with the collection. The collection in the pavilion is not Byzantine at all. It's South American. Actually, it's pre-Columbian.

So you picked the form simply because it appealed to you?

I was always passionate about Mimar Sinan, and the idea of using those little domes, which is Arab or Islamic. And then the nine squares made perfect circulation. I don't know where things come from. I used the drums before that at Yale in the Kline Science Center – the Tootsie Roll building.

The Tootsie Roll building?

All my buildings have these silly names – like the Lipstick building. It was the students, naturally, who came up with the name the Tootsie Roll building.

Did your interest in Sinan come out of your travels? For example,

The minute you take an inside view you see what the idea is. It's a purely "inside" building. It has no facades at all.

were there particular buildings done in that style that you were interested in?

Yes. I was inspired by the Madrasa [school] across the street from Sinan's great mosque in Istanbul – it looked very much like this. In fact, the idea of clustered domes came straight from Istanbul. And, of course, it didn't hurt that Dumbarton Oaks is a Byzantine institute.
It's hard for me to remember how the layering came about, but of course, I had both in mind, the main collection and the

Pre-Columbian collection – although I knew it was for South American objects. But I thought they might enjoy the Byzantine.

But even if this had been, let's say, an early American collection, you were interested in using those forms at that time?

Yes, I was. But you see, the building is not meant to be looked at from the outside. It's not really a building that would cause you to say, "Oh, there's an interesting building." But the minute you take an inside view you see what the idea is. It's a purely "inside" building. It has no facades at all. The Madrasa had none; all you could see were the floating domes over the walls. I would have had to use a wall if it hadn't been in the woods.

Did the neighborhood or local preservation group have a lot of input into the design?

The association didn't bother me because the building wasn't facing the street. It was fine as long as you kept it back in the woods and didn't make it high or anything. What could they say?

You've said this was your most interesting project. Is it your favorite project as well?

It was of that period.

Is it because of the way it turned out or because of the process? You mentioned that Mrs. Bliss was a wonderful person.

She was a wonderful backer. I said, "I can't fit that function in. Why don't we put it in the basement?" That's where everything

> There was no budget. No budget at all. The critic Peter Blake once figured out it was the most expensive building per square foot ever built.

practical is, of course. She should have said, "Now, here's your program for this house." Normally, the program is, there are so many square feet for offices, so many square feet for a library, and it would have left a little museum somewhere. I said, "Oh, you'll take care of all that, won't you? We'll make a beautiful gallery."

So all of the services and everything else are underneath?

It's appalling down there because it's so small and cramped. What was so good about this project was that I was left alone to

work very hard on the monumental. See, all the horrors you have to have, spotlights, and the fire protection system, are all in that grid, so you don't see them. I was free in those days, and Mrs. Bliss was so appreciative. There was no budget. No budget at all. The critic Peter Blake once figured out it was the most expensive building per square foot ever built.

Well, one article said that it was about $160 to $180 per square foot – in 1963.

When buildings were costing $50 for 3,000 feet.

We were wondering about the idea of procession in the building. Did you use any ideas relating to procession from either the Amon Carter Museum or the Sheldon Memorial Art Gallery?

This was entirely separate, but it's very processional. At least you're not going to have to double back. No dead ends.

We had heard that the original design for the entrance to the museum was going to be different, but there was an oak tree in the way.

It was a marvelous tree that was in the way, and so we put it a little farther away from the building. I said, "Well, we're not going to touch that tree." We all agreed.

Were the doors that surround the fountain courtyard meant to be fixed, or did you want them opened or closed?

No, closed.

We found the echo effect utterly fascinating.

Oh, isn't that marvelous? I knew that would happen, but I didn't know what fun it would be. You almost don't see the objects.

Well, it makes you self-conscious because you feel like you are on a public address system.

All domes do that. I knew it would happen. It was mostly criticized: "How could you build a building when you knew it was going to have terribly bad acoustics?"

We thought part of the idea was that in this museum you should look at the art, be quiet, and listen to the fountain.

Sure, that's all. It is a place to look at objects. And these rooms are small enough so you can. If you put these objects in a great big museum, they'd be lost. Wouldn't be there at all. But it is intimate, about the size of a living room, or smaller than a living room – you have more fun. But that was the deep criticism of it.

The other criticism was that it is not a nighttime building. It's awful at night.

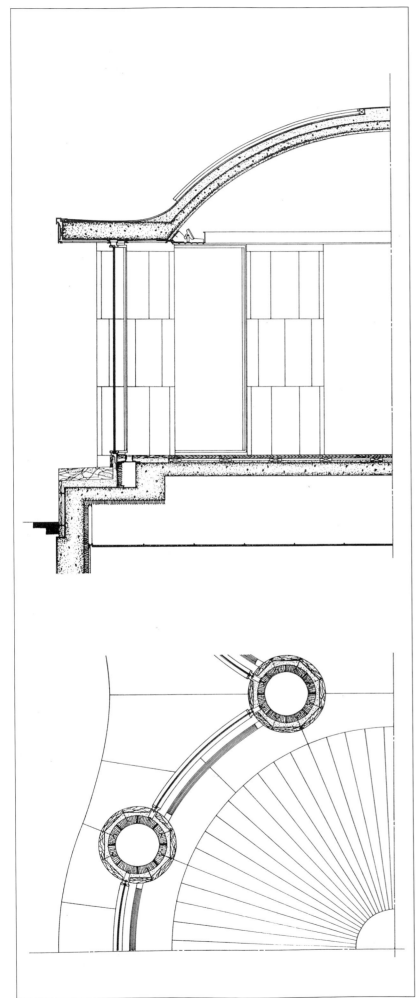

SECTIONAL FLOOR PLAN AND ELEVATION

Did you design it with the idea in mind that there would be only a couple visitors at a time?

Yes, it was never "popular" as a museum; it wasn't meant to be. It's a scholarly institution. Harvard took it over. The president of Harvard [Derek Bok] said, "Oh, I'll send my engineers down; we'll fix all that," meaning the echo caused by the domes.

In an article from the A.I.A. Journal of 1964, the building is called "postmodern." What's your reaction to that?

Well, it doesn't make any difference to me. That was after I taught at Yale, you see, where I said, "You cannot not know history." I was always historically minded. And that had a lot to do with Bob Stern and everybody's thing in the 1970s.
I guess that's right. It crossed my mind.

In your work there's always a bit of classicism.

Always a bit of something. All Mies's work is classical. And even though we don't realize it now, modern has become just exactly the opposite. All we say now is, "My God, that's awful; it's classical." Well, that's reasonably new. Le Corbusier, look at his notebooks; he was very classically minded.

Don't you find it surprising that people are just coming to terms with that now? Why in, let's say, 1970, did critics not recognize publicly that these works were classical?

In Dumbarton Oaks the axis is classical, of course. And the domes are Islamic. But I think you can do anything you want. To me they were just new. I never thought about where I got things from. Afterwards, interviewers and people all want labels, so then I remembered Sinan, but to me, it was just in part an Islamic collection. And Mrs. Bliss was just delighted that I thought of that.

Robert Stern had mentioned Frank Lloyd Wright as an influence in an article in 1980.

Influence over me? Really? Anything's possible. Do you think it was the use of circles in the building? Like that house I did on Nantucket. But I don't see Dumbarton Oaks in that connection; that's not possible.

Well, Frank Lloyd Wright isn't classical.

Oh, look at his museum in Milwaukee. Ionic columns. Or the Blossom House. Oh, no, he's much more all over the place than one talks about.

The Guggenheim Museum is a wonderful example of a building based on the circle. Was there a certain period where architects were looking more at circular forms?

Oh, yes. That came up in my consciousness, also with the Jester House, Wright's round house. I was amazed to see the circle in that. It's when I was working on the house in Nantucket.

Why do you think that the circle was either so out of fashion or just out of use for so long? It's not the most practical form, but it has always been the most sacred.

A hopelessly impractical form except for a temple. But this isn't about circles; this is a classical square. I wonder if it isn't more Soane? A small round room.

Taken one dome at a time, it feels more like Soane. But with your composition, the immediate effect is very Islamic.

Islamic architects would never have designed a nine-dome composition. There was really no attempt on my part to study Islamic architecture. I just remembered that the feeling of repeated domes was a rather delicious way to organize space in a module. It's modular.

It reminded us in a strange way of your pavilion in New Canaan.

Yes, very modular.

And here you're also dealing with turning the corner using the column. Yet one column is with squares and one is with circles.

But the principle is the same, and that was in Mondrian, overall, which is classical. I mean, you expected it came from Hadrian, although it didn't. Well, there's a little Hadrian in it. His little room in Tivoli was circular.

So Dumbarton Oaks is sort of eight Temple of Vestas connected?

Yes it is. It's funny, you'd think it would be hard to think of, wouldn't you? See, no architect knows what happens at that point. It's impossible to know what influences from your early life or from study are up in your consciousness.

But you were interested in that type of form, the specific commission was not necessarily the point?

Sure.

If you liked it so much, why didn't you build something similar on your own property? Is it because once you've done a project, it's time to move on?

Yes. Time to move on.

You said that Mrs. Bliss was a wonderful patron to work with. What were her interests?

Arts. It was her husband who was the collector, but the building didn't interest him. She was a can-do sort of a person. But her main interest was flowers, gardens, and mine wasn't. I first met her through Jack Thatcher, and I was presold, of course. Lincoln Kirstein introduced me to Jack Thatcher. At first, Mrs. Bliss was very polite and grande dame-ish. It wasn't until she started seeing the shapes that she really got interested in the model. If I had a strong approach that she didn't understand, she'd just say, "Well, you're the architect."

You were happy about that.

I never thought of it. I thought that's the way you did architecture, like at the Seagram Building. So I said, "Well, architecture is a rather good profession."

Do you think it's fair to say that given a greater budget most architecture could be improved? Is it better to have a client that says, "Here are the checks. Do what you have to do."

But you'd better pick a good architect. A lousy architect could spend the money, and you still get a very bad building. A very fancy bad building. Like a lot of Newport houses – even the great Biltmore is not such a good piece of architecture. But to Frank Lloyd Wright, you should do that. Write the checks as you go along, because then he would have done great works.

How long did it take you to complete the design? Is this an idea that you had in the back of your mind and therefore were able to do very quickly?

Very quickly. You usually have to do it four or five times, and I simply don't remember. I know now it takes months. Once that happens, then the rest is coasting. I built it very, very easily.

Are there any specific details in the building of which you are particularly fond?

Well, there are the circles and the way they were handled and also the floor. There was no rosette up in the domes – no lantern. The dome was not used at all in the Renaissance way, you see. I used it as a way of putting a ceiling in, so there's no centering device, and yet there is this very symmetrical passage, symmetrical in every way.

Did you consider putting anything in the center of the ceiling? Or did you like the idea of a blank ceiling?

Never at Dumbarton Oaks. Well, the first time I did this with a dome was my remodeling in my place in the country. And I did that with a little light in the center. I mean, you've got to have something to mark the center. But I took it out. Then we used the floor pattern as the theme.

I think that there's a quote in one of the old articles on the museum that says that the dome represents the sky.

That old wheeze, it never crossed my mind. I'll tell you where I spent most of my time – on the connection. It only shows in the plan. All these things came to me: How do you handle that, because everything is reversed? You see, if you're standing where

It's quite amusing. I didn't have to do toilets. I didn't have to do a door or a coat closet or an information desk.

the plant is, the walls are all coming out at you. So I did plan the plants to obstruct the view.

So the plants become almost structural?

They work like a wall, to keep you always looking one way, to have you start feeling that you might get through there. I had the same problem in my little pavilion on the lake. One way was forbidden, although it was pretty easy to step across that. Well, I simply wouldn't let guests do it. With the plants I am saying, I'm sorry, you have to go *this* way.

Follow the colored line?

Follow the colored line, and you ought to know the rules by now. But here you can't go the wrong way; it's more successful.

Was there anything else that was difficult to design?

Well, another thing that didn't work – it's always fun to think of things that didn't work – was the connections: Where do you start this thing?

You wanted the building to be closer to the main building?

Yes, it was closer originally.

Did you consider just making it a separate pavilion?

Yes. They didn't think that was very funny. I would have preferred that.

It would be a pavilion then, just like in New Canaan.

That's right. But how do you make a connection to a pavilion? This has no beginning or end. When you go into that Madrasa in

Istanbul, you just walk into the court. Yes, that was never solved. You have to have some failures.

And then you chose the way that the trees were to be planted around it?

No, no. Well, I did say you've got to do the hollies here, because you see a wall. But, of course, the hollies at once dropped their leaves on the side I wanted the leaves on.

Because there's no sun on that side.

No sun on that side, so then it gets bare. I couldn't change nature very well.

One other thing that they had mentioned was that in the little walkway between the buildings, birds fly into the glass in the springtime and drop dead.

They do it in my house, too. Oh, well, they've learned. It took them about 35 years. You know, well, I just get one or two in the season now.

If you could, would you change anything, other than not having the entrance where it is?

No, but you see, weren't they nice not to make me do a stairway to the offices? It's quite amusing. I didn't have to do toilets. I didn't have to do a door or a coat closet or an information desk. How could you imagine a better program?

It's a little temple?

A little temple. Except there's nothing religious about it. It's more like a madrasa than a mosque.
That front door – there isn't supposed to be an entrance; there isn't supposed to be an accent. I mean, that's what's unclassical and un-nineteenth century about it. You just walk directly into the first circle.

It is more high Renaissance. The focus is still on the center.

Right. Maybe if we did it now, we'd have a diagonal.

Mrs. Bliss was very pleased?

Oh, she just loved it. She was sympathetic.

Why do you think it's so hard to find clients like that now? There are people who have money.

I would say most people don't like art. They're more interested in other things, like money making or something. It's odd to me.

FOUNTAIN COURT AS VIEWED FROM MUSEUM INTERIOR

In 1953, Philip Johnson built one of his best-known works: the sculpture garden at The Museum of Modern Art. MoMA had a garden that dated from 1939, which Johnson then extensively remodeled in order to exhibit effectively the works chosen by Alfred Barr, the museum's first director. Johnson himself describes this garden not as a landscape but as a room in which sculpture can be well displayed and city dwellers can enjoy the outdoors.

A mixture of architecture and landscape, the sculpture garden is considered to be one of the great examples of modern landscape design. The spaces are all laid out so as to have many rooms within the larger one, which can only be reached by certain paths. Like Johnson's own garden at his house on Ash Street, a wall isolates the garden from the street. The garden is used by visitors to the museum and for special events. It is one of Johnson's favorite – and most popular – public spaces.

Johnson, a former director of the Department of Architecture and Design at MoMA, understood the problems that museums encountered presenting sculpture. Johnson's garden is a solution to the challenge of exhibiting sculpture and painting in a way that highlights the object without subjecting it to the competing vistas of other visual works. Johnson would go on to provide a very different solution in his own sculpture gallery in New Canaan, Connecticut.

At what point did The Museum of Modern Art decide that it was going to have a sculpture garden? Was that a long-standing interest of the museum?

Oh, no, that was done back with John McAndrew and Alfred Barr. Nelson Rockefeller wanted to save something for his mother, to honor her. He knew the other Rockefellers would help to pitch in. Oh, this was another case where I had a good client.

He said, "Do the garden. We're not talking so much about budget, but we'd like to have a permanent, nice garden there." So we did it.

Did the museum originally want it so that the public could just walk in, like a vest-pocket park?

Oh, no, impossible, because they had to charge for the museum. But Nelson was worried about the people across the street. We had put up a great big wall.

It's like an urban version of your Ash Street house; it is essentially a court-house.

It's a court-house. I took it from a Catholic institution of some kind located on 70-something street here in New York that has an even higher wall. So I said to Nelson, "We have this wall as in any institution that's private, any monastery. Why do you think the wall is too long?" And he said, "Well, this isn't 70-something Street. This is a valuable piece of downtown New York real estate. We've got people who live across the street and we just can't do that to them."

So we put in the gate, but we succeeded anyhow, because we had very, very deep louvers, so people don't gather there. You can't get enough of an angle to see in. Try to peek in. You can't. That's the way we have to trick our clients. But they didn't mind when the garden was opened.

Is this a project that you're particularly fond of?

Oh, yes, this is the one that gives me a reputation for being a better landscape architect than I am an architect.

And you like that?

I don't mind at all; it is all the same art. Except my knowledge of plant material is lacking, so I had very good advisers.

Did you pick the placement for the sculptures?

No, that was Alfred and his people.

You use water prominently in this garden, and yet aren't there problems with water?

It leaks.

If you designed it today, would you still use the water?

I would still use the water. It's much too important here, as it is in the great square in Peking. It's just a matter of maintenance and money.

The garden's design still has the sliding planes of Mies.

Oh, yes, you're right about that. It is an urban garden surrounded with a wall, like a monastery. This is a sculpture garden. My main interest was none of that – it was the question of obstacle and circulation. You see, I had five different areas. All of them have a different shape. And how do you divide them? Well, I used water as the device to divide and connect at the same time. It makes separate areas for installation. The most fun was picking what was to go in the islands.

If you had the garden completely open the way the museum did in the 1939 plan, you couldn't put anywhere near as much sculpture in as you can here.

Here you have separate outdoor rooms.

That's right. These are outdoor rooms that then have constrictions. Like this island here with greenery all carefully closed in.

The second idea of great importance was the stairs, and that, of course, has been ruined. The most important thing is you look down. Alfred asked me one day, "Philip, why is it that the garden looks bigger than it did before?" I said, "Because we go down now." See, if you make a scoop of something, then that increases your apparent length.

Was the terrace originally designed for eating?

That's right. It's a summer place.

The terrace was a containment for the eaters to keep them from dribbling out into the garden. I wanted to create the intimacy of a green edge, you see. If you know you could eat all over the terrace, you're not contained. Same as in the Glass House. Without the little granite edge, you're not contained from the view. Aesthetically, you leak, and I didn't want any leakage that way. I wanted a definite place.

What was the reaction of the neighbors when this wall was put up along 54th Street?

They said, "Well, look, you planted nicely in the garden; what about planting something in the street? Look, it's very nice for you, but we just have a blank wall." And of course, the building across the street is called Rockefeller Apartments; you know, Nelson built that.

Well, it is perfectly lovely if you're up there and you look down on the garden.

That's right.

In your original design for the garden, there seems to be a little area of light passing through between the marble panels, almost like those in the Boston Public Library. Sort of a peek-through.

Oh, yes. Well, I didn't like mortar there. But the mortar isn't there anymore.

Was this project fun to do?

Well, my main boss was René d'Harnoncourt, the director of the museum. He was a closer friend of Nelson than I was, so I'd get things filtered through his skillful Viennese eyes. That was a great thing. And then the redo was truly wonderful under David Rockefeller.

Did you have input on Museum Tower?

Museum Tower, no. They didn't give it to me to build. I was furious, and they were furious at me. I don't know what for; they wouldn't tell me. An architect only builds a few years for any institution and then he loses his credibility.

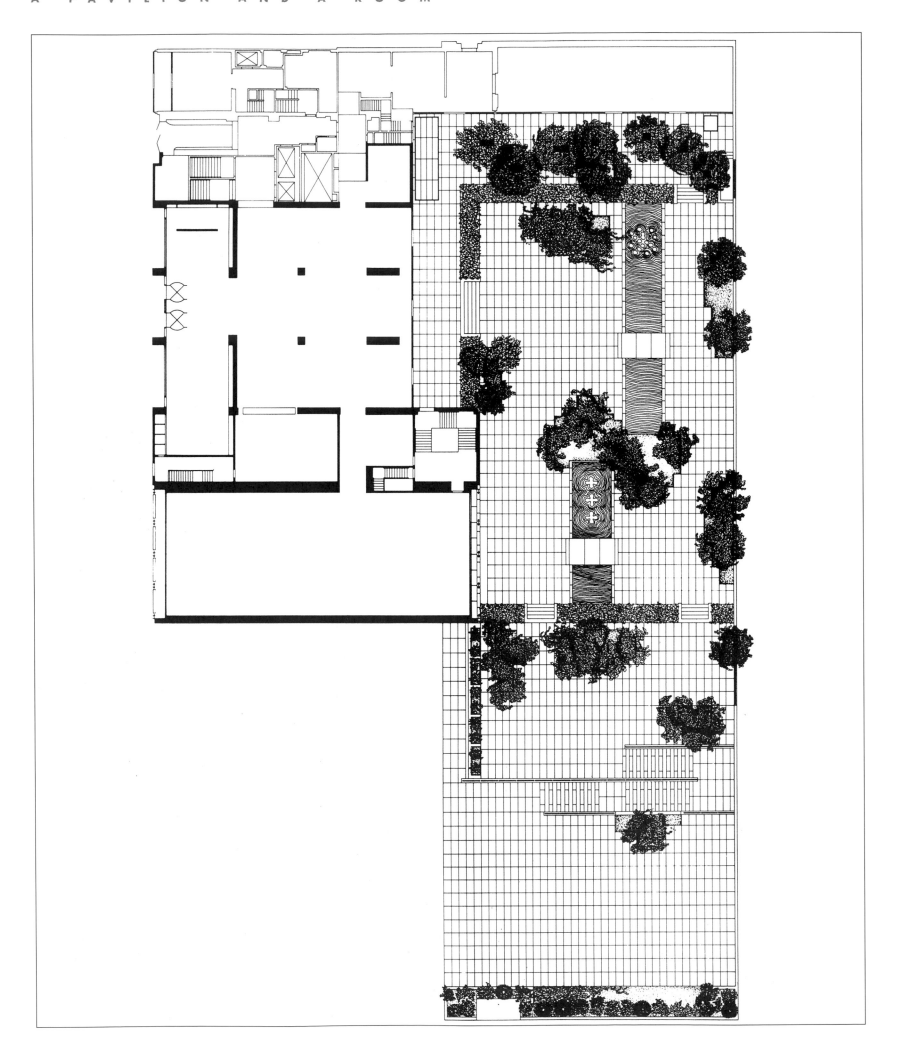

SCULPTURE GARDEN, ORIGINAL PLAN

They didn't even ask you?

Never asked me. Well, Blanchette Rockefeller fell in love with another architect, but I didn't have anything to do with it at all. It was very nice because I was busy with other things.

You are very interested in landscape architecture. Was this one of your first projects where you were really doing landscape design?

But this is a room, not a garden. It's an urban room with definite doorways and processionals. And yet it's easy enough to penetrate. If you're not forced to move that way and this way, you won't see anything. So you always see a lot of sculpture. You say, "I wonder what's behind over there a little bit?" It has to be enough to entice you to go back there.

Is it at its best when there are very few people in the garden or when there are a lot?

It's better to have few, of course, because then you get the feeling of the space. But it can take solid crowds.

It actually disperses crowds rather well as opposed to, say, an open space where there's no way to hide.

That's right. Now here you can say, "Let's go across the canal. We can have a little talk."

Often buildings in New York have a separate room or an atrium or a plaza attached to them. Your design was fairly early for that in New York. Do you think this was something that people later looked at as a model?

No, it's not an atrium in any sense, because it's not a place where you cut across and then have something else happening on the other side.

This is a backyard.

Yes, and it helps enormously to have put all the windows here.

It gives you a permanent light court.

Yes.

What was there before you built the sculpture garden?

That was the backyard of Mrs. Rockefeller's house. Mrs. Rockefeller had lived right there. They moved out, so they tore the house down. I was a director at MoMA at the time when the garden was first built.

Was there anything that you saved from that garden design?

Nothing. I saved absolutely nothing. Quite the opposite, I cut down quite a few of their trees. That made Alfred Barr furious. But I said to him, "Alfred, trees you can replace, but this is a room and it has to last a long time." I cut down one tree that was right in the wrong place. A tree in the wrong place is a weed. Imagine having the power that I had, that I could cut down a tree in New York City!

Couldn't do that today.

Not then either. But if your name is Rockefeller, you can do quite a few things. It was faith on his part, you see. The important thing is that a client has to have faith. It's terrible to cut the tree, but we replaced it with a lot of other trees.

You discuss Mr. Rockefeller as the client, but in fact the museum was the client. Was it very difficult having to deal with a committee of people?

Committees!

Wasn't there a committee?

No, how could there be a committee? No, I don't work with committees. We're doing over the front of the museum now – the

But this is a room, not a garden. It's an urban room with definite doorways and processionals. And yet it's easy enough to penetrate.

lobby is so awful – and they said, "Why don't you do it?" I said, "I will." And they said, "Well, come to the committee meeting." I went, and I'm not going to touch it.

So there was no institutional committee to deal with?

None. I talked with Alfred about everything, because he was my best friend, and with René. Nelson I seldom saw, but he trusted René and me.

That's the best situation. Did this project whet your appetite for landscaping?

No, I was already doing landscape in the country. That's still going on. The best way to landscape, you take 40 years, and then see what you need.

Forty years is just a drop in the bucket.

A drop in the bucket in landscaping, surely. Poor Le Nôtre, he never got to see how wonderful his gardens were.

The tall, slender quality of the different walls is reminiscent of the Barcelona Pavilion.

Mies wasn't building a single room though. But in the garden that was a good idea: the rooms and the water. You have to connect but separate.

Did you go through many different designs to end up with the finished product?

The question always comes up. I don't remember. I simply don't remember. I remember an awful lot of sketch paper and throwing it away.

Did you have input on exactly which sculpture was coming into the garden? Or was that all Alfred Barr's responsibility?

All Alfred. It had to be flexible, because they change the exhibits so often.

Well, it's one of the most popular spaces in New York.

It costs $7 to get in, so it's not too popular.

You need a place to relax after looking at all that artwork. You're so relieved that there is no painting to focus on.

You can go out in the summer and you can have a drink.

Do you think that it is inappropriate for a museum or a cultural institution to have a popular cafe or restaurant?

The Modern is very much against it. The best one is in Milan in their big museum, the Brera. There you go through endless things, but then you come to the place where they serve you something to drink. It's just what you want, but it doesn't take up a lot of room. You see, Alfred Barr and I didn't like that the area on the first floor is all taken up by food. The food gets mixed up with the art.

And that area is a wonderful space. Of course, Alfred was always eager to get his hands on more space. If they would use it like they do in Milan it would be better. "Oh, I'm getting museum fatigue." You stop and have a Campari. But you could look out at the city at the same time. At the Metropolitan Museum of Art you could have those in little places. Areas of rest.

I think that should be done on the third floor of the Modern. Just a little bar for coffee in the morning: have some espresso — let's go. It's European, you see, and Americans don't know

enough. It wouldn't pay for itself, of course, but it doesn't pay for itself, that big restaurant.

Well, have you mentioned the idea of an espresso bar to people at the museum?

No. The Modern is an entirely different place now. Too many committees.

When you first began your work at the Modern, what were the expectations?

Alfred knew what the Modern wanted to do. It was very clear and the trustees trusted him. The head of the trustees was Abby

If they would use it like they do in Milan it would be better. "Oh, I'm getting museum fatigue." You stop and have a Campari.

Aldrich Rockefeller, who had the energy of a wildcat. She just had a will of iron, and she forced everything through. We knew we had complete backing.

Alfred Barr was her genius scholar. He couldn't run a museum, but that didn't appear until later. And of course, with those great shows he had, he couldn't go wrong. It was very popular right from the beginning.

So it was immediately accepted?

Immediately. Well, accepted by enough people so that we couldn't stay at the Heckscher Building because we ruined the elevator system. We had to go somewhere. So we went to the house that the Rockefellers owned here.

Modernism is viewed as this wonderful force of the avant garde. Yet if you look at who supported modern art in the United States, you will find that the people almost without exception came from the most established sectors of society.

We're just looking for their successors now.

It's hard to find them?

I haven't had any luck. I think it goes in cycles; it's hard to say. I think it was all an accident of the time – that Mrs. Rockefeller was interested in modern art. There was a pent-up need because of the attitude, the stupid attitude of the Metropolitan Museum of Art that never found Cézanne at all.

The Met's come around a little bit since.

Oh, yes, they're doing much better.

Do you think that it's foolish for a museum to treat its architecture as sacrosanct? In other words, as if to say, "We cannot put an addition on the original. Let's build a separate pavilion; let's build an addition as a separate building."

Of course, you can add to any building. Christopher Wren added to the Tudor building at Hampton Court – he had to. It didn't bother anybody.

Is it different when you're working with a modern building?

I made an addition to the regular MoMA building. It doesn't look funny at all. Wren must have looked very funny to Henry VIII. So what!

So you think museums are being too fussy about putting additions on their original buildings? Do you think Michael Graves's Whitney Museum project should have gone forward?

Of course that should have. It's too late. They had a moment there where they could have done it. Well, they said it wasn't fair to the Breuer building. What's not fair to what building in New York? In fact, a little difference makes the block jollier. I almost like the new building more than Breuer's anyhow. Of course, that made all the old Breuer people upset.

So you don't think there's anything particularly sacrosanct about a modern building that stands as its own object?

No, the sin that Michael Graves did was to impinge on the old building with that swivel that covered one little bay of the Breuer building. Oh, his idea was good.

How do you feel about the new Guggenheim addition?

That's good. The great part about Wright was the room, the big room. That looks much better than it did before. Oh, it never hurts to play with a building.

When MoMA was first being constructed, did you have any input into the building?

I left the Modern just before that, but Alfred kept in touch with me. He said, "Would you mind just penning a few lines?" So I did but I didn't change it much. You can't do that.

This was before you went to architectural school?

Yes. Only a critic in those days.

Building for City and State

New York State Theater, Lincoln Center
New York, New York
1964

Boston Public Library Addition
Boston, Massachusetts
1966-1973

Johnson and a group of prominent architects were brought together by Governor Nelson Rockefeller in the early 1960s to design the Lincoln Center for the Performing Arts in New York City. Johnson originally suggested a colonnade to enclose the U-shaped court of the troika of the Metropolitan Opera House, Avery Fisher Hall, and the New York State Theater. While this grand scheme was not carried out, his idea for the plaza and fountain, taken from Michelangelo's Capitoline Hill (Campidoglio) in Rome, was followed.

Johnson's original design for the commission, the New York State Theater, in fact dated back to the 1950s. He had been hired to create a "Theater of Dance": a home for the New York City Ballet, which was then the fiefdom of the creative master, George Balanchine, and run by Johnson's close friend, Lincoln Kirstein.

In his final design, the theater became two main spaces: the auditorium and the grand promenade. The richness of the materials was unusual for the mid-1960s, when poured concrete was the material of choice. Johnson selected travertine for the floor, gold leaf for the ceiling, and bronze for the railings that surround the balconies in the promenade. Johnson's unabashed combination of opulence and historical forms sent shock waves through architectural circles and the viewing public.

Was the overall plan of three buildings for Lincoln Center originally your idea, and did you organize the work of the other architects involved in the project?

I was influential on two things, the use of travertine and the 24-foot module. We all used the same module since the buildings were all for the same type of purpose and shouldn't have been different heights. This gave unity to the whole square.

That we all managed to agree was very hard for the seven or so architects involved. But since they were all so split up and my idea of how to group the buildings was so simple, nobody's ego was too badly smashed by agreeing to my plan.

Personally, I wanted my building, the New York State Theater, to be north of there, on the next block where the Juilliard School is now. The design was a half-circle that was to face the diagonal of Broadway. But they put me on the same site with the other buildings and I accepted that. I had no influence on the others, really, but I did do the plaza.

When we look at it, we certainly see Michelangelo's Campidoglio.

Of course, it's quite obvious.

Originally, you were going to close off the plaza with an arcade.

I was going to put my arcade right around and then just glue the three buildings onto the arcade, if you can imagine. Wally Harri-

son said, "Philip, who do you think is going to let you put an arcade right across the front of all their buildings?" The other two architects didn't see why they should build behind my arcade. My attempt to take over. We all tried to. Everyone was pushing for lead position.

When did you complete the theater?

I'll tell you, the day President Kennedy was shot in 1963, I was there, and the building still wasn't finished. But we did open it six months later. Now I don't know when the Opera House was opened; it was much later, I think. Harrison had more trouble finishing the Opera House.

The theater has a very different interior from those of the Metropolitan Opera House and Avery Fisher Hall, despite any similarities on the exteriors.

Well, Mr. Abramovitz was a very different kind of architect. To me, in Avery Fisher Hall he wasted all his extra space down on the sides. I'd rather gather up all that cubage and put it in the

Lincoln Kirstein and I didn't pay any attention when Max Abramovitz said that you have to have a certain proportion of the hall to the foyer area. We did whatever we wanted.

front. But he didn't have the committee's will either – to have the chance to have a front room. I'm the only one who had that.

Why not? He didn't have as many square feet as you did?

He already had too big a proportion of his usable to unusable space. Lincoln Kirstein and I didn't pay any attention when Max Abramovitz said that you have to have a certain proportion of the hall to the foyer area. We did whatever we wanted.

Abramovitz took a lot of space to go all the way down the side corridors, which are empty because there are only a few people who go down there. In my design, I just gathered up those two spaces and put them in front. I don't know that I have more or less space than there is in Avery Fisher Hall or the Opera House, but I do have a room.

Were you thinking of any distinct models when you were putting the design together?

Yes, I was thinking of eighteenth-century theaters. I was also looking at specific books on theaters, in particular, a German book on the history of theaters, "modern" theaters. It was by Gottfried Semper, I think. The book ended with his work in Dresden and Vienna. Of course, I also looked at Charles Garnier, the architect of the Paris Opera House.

When we first looked at the Theater, we felt it was so French, and yet it also feels German.

More French. The Germans of the eighteenth century were French-speaking; all the elite were.

The interior also seems very moderne. It's almost a 1930s or a 1940s feeling.

You're absolutely right. It couldn't be more eighteenth century because we lack the crafts today, nor did I want it to be. But by keeping the many balconies, I thought that would be enough. The rest is just moderne. Yet I wanted to go back. This was in the period when I was deep enough into revivals to do that, and so you'll find a mixture there in the hall itself.

Tell us a little bit about how you developed the form in the ceiling. It looks rather floral.

No, it's like the paving in the plaza.

From Michelangelo's Campidoglio?

I have used it a number of times. I had a carpet over 50-feet long with the same pattern in the old office.

Was the ceiling design done for acoustical purposes?

Oh, Lord, yes. It's all open, and then the acoustic adjustments are above, hidden by the mesh.

The lights and the central fixture almost seem like jewelry decorating the room.

That's what it's supposed to be. Good for you, you read it in my intentions and those of Dick Kelly, the man who really founded modern lighting. They are supposed to be faceted diamonds. They're faceted all right, but they don't do the same thing as a cut piece of glass. We call them the "headlights." We hoped they would be like crystals – sparkle. But we had to do it in plastic, of course, and it didn't sparkle. Faceting doesn't work well with plastic, because plastic doesn't act like glass.

Why not use glass? Would it have been too heavy, or too expensive?

Expensive.

ACOUSTICAL CEILING IN THE THEATER

Were budget factors a major problem?

No, but the whole thing was expensive, and New York State was paying for it. I was very lucky because I had good clients, Nelson Rockefeller and Lincoln Kirstein.

The floor in the auditorium seems to be just colored concrete. Was that done for an aesthetic purpose or to cut costs?

Well, we didn't want to use that originally. I think we ended up using it because of something about cutting the auditorium's acoustic absorption.

We were fascinated by the choice of materials.

Oh, those were delightful. I took a long time on those.

Tell us about the bronze panels in the grand promenade. How were those designed?

They were very hard to do. I found a little shop down in Greenwich Village, and they were made right there. The people there didn't really know what they were doing. They just laid these things down and welded the bronze. We got the individuality of the panels with no high technology. In the great old days, you had somebody who knew how to do that, but not today. So I said, "Let's do what we can." The texture was what we got, semi-accidental blobs of brass stuck to the woven wires.

It looks almost like a Jackson Pollock.

Pure accident.

What about the choice of sculpture in the theater?

The sculpture is an emotional thing because Lincoln Kirstein was very fond of the sculptor, Elie Nadelman. I have one in the Glass House. Nelson Rockefeller had one. The original is only five-feet high. We had these copies blown up in Carrara, Italy. We had to take a window out to get them in. Everybody just hated them: "Big fat nude women in a perfectly decent hall." It's funny how things melt into the history, isn't it?

We read somewhere that people were saying that there was a sinister quality to the sculpture.

But it's just delightful. The girls with little martinis, having a good time. Well, that's what I think the theme is. Joyful.

And the ceiling is covered with 22-karat gold leaf?

Yes, gold leaf. We had a little bit of extra money and put it toward the ceiling.

Why didn't you choose to hang any chandeliers from the ceiling?

Well, there still aren't any good chandeliers. If you use chandeliers as a source of light, that's the very worst kind of lighting. So I couldn't use them for light. Also, I couldn't get really good ones – oh, I could, of course, if I had them made in Vienna. But the cost was fantastic, and I didn't want to emphasize the ceiling in that way. This was an entirely different approach, so I just decided not to use them.

Where does the light emanate from?

The walls, indirect lighting.

The best critic is, of all people, Virgil Thomson, the famous music critic. He said, "Philip Johnson's interiors always look as if he got them from jails." And you know, that's exactly where I got it. If you visit a good jail, it would look like this. They're usually much narrower, but the little cells are off the balconies. You can always watch where everybody is, you see. There are some charming interiors of jails.

The only one I visited at that time was H. H. Richardson's big jail in Pittsburgh, the Allegheny Courthouse. But I always liked that shape of a semi-enclosure. Here I left out the wall on the north side.

We noticed another sort of Richardsonian effect in the way the wall from the theater juts out.

Yes, and it makes that bulge. I didn't think of that as Richardsonian. Oh, on the other hand, that's right, like the stairway walls in the libraries.

In other words, when you're in the promenade, you immediately know which direction the auditorium is, even though the room is rectangular.

You know where you are, obviously. When I got that idea, I felt much better because it obviously made something out of this "jail." It's similar to my work in the Bobst Library for New York University

How did you come up with the design of the staircases? They're such wonderful shapes; they seem like 1930s French design.

Yes, that's exactly what they are. However, they are more nineteenth century although, of course, I was thinking in terms of baroque stairways. Everything there is travertine. The floor is travertine except for the red marble.

Would that room be hard to do today because it would be so expensive to build?

Yes, indeed, it's the handwork. The people who can carve it are the Italians. You could get plenty of them from Italy in those days.

So you don't think that it is possible to get great carving done today? What about the incredible carving in the addition to the Jewish Museum on Fifth Avenue?

Well, you still can do it; it's just a question of money and time and finding the people. I would never think of doing that, building an addition that is an exact match, because it's no fun. Where can you get your kicks?

Can you tell us about the other art in the public places of the theater? We noticed a beautiful Jasper Johns on the main floor.

That's my choice. It's called *Numbers*. It's done in Sculpmetal, which is very difficult stuff to use. It's the only thing that's become

Virgil Thomson, the famous music critic, said, "Philip Johnson's interiors always look as if he got them from jails."

thing that's become valuable. It's very amusing. I never knew Jasper was going to be such a success.

All of the art in the theater is refreshingly modern for a performance hall. When you see it you know that you are in New York, down the street from MoMA. You are not in Europe. Did you choose all the other sculpture?

I chose all the art, but I also had committees and donors. Mrs. John D. Rockefeller III gave me the Jacques Lipschitz piece at the end of the long corridor. I commissioned the Lee Bontecou.

Compared with the other buildings of Lincoln Center, this building has a greater sense of classicism and procession of space.

Yes, that's me. Classicism. My principle was you can't reinvent the spoon. If you want a festival theater where you want to see and be seen, a theater where you go to have some sort of a ceremony, how are you going to beat the eighteenth century?

Now I had one twentieth-century problem: I had to accommodate a lot of seats. The balcony can be a very unpleasant place. Less costly seats and perfect acoustics. But there are some bad seats up there because of the angle of vision. From there you can only see the front dancers, and you look at them like mice. Those seats are also empty in La Scala. But I wanted to have the bands of the balconies go all the way around. Form was more important than function by a good deal. I wasn't trying to be original at all at the New York State Theater. My kick was getting this lobby and the ring of seats.

The lobby is really the "see and be seen" portion of the theater. Can you tell us about the curtains? We were fascinated by the beaded metal you chose.

Well, it came from the curtains at the Seagram Building, the Four Seasons, of course. They worked so well there that I couldn't do louvered ones. People like to touch them. If they tear off, you put another one up. You see, being round, the little balls catch the light, so they are always lighted. You can push them apart to walk through them.

What was your reaction when you first attended an evening performance after the building was completed?

It worked. The only thing that doesn't work is that they don't promenade in a circle the way they should, as they do in Paris. All Europeans understand the promenade and walk in the same direction. It's just marvelous, because then you can see everyone who is walking on the other side. Well, it's like the streets of a little Italian town. There they promenade at certain times. They don't promenade in American lobbies.

But you could have a drink maybe, unless you're too busy.

Too busy making their efforts at meeting Mrs. Important or something. But the room is big enough to do that, you see. You can get around the node all right, even with the entire audience out here. Yes, I remember being there lots of times – I've been there for dinners too. It's a good place for events.

So when you were there for the first time, your only disappointment was that the theatergoers wouldn't promenade properly?

Oh, that wasn't much of a disappointment. No, it's hardly a disappointment to have people filling that room.

How did you originally get involved with the project? Did Lincoln Kirstein contact you early on?

Yes. There were several false starts, of course. Lincoln had the idea we'd put it in Central Park. Just behind the gold statue there off 59th Street.

Was all of Lincoln Center to go there too?

No, no. Lincoln Center hadn't been invented yet.

Did the overall conception of Lincoln Center come after you had been chosen to do the New York State Theater?

Yes, long after. Originally I wasn't concerned with it at all. I saw it from the prints the newspapers made of what Wally Harrison was suggesting. It didn't include the theater at that time. And then it went over into politics with Nelson Rockefeller, who was the governor. He was very fond of Lincoln. He was closer to Lincoln than he was to me. So it all sort of happened. And then of course the battles were so awful, we mostly got discouraged.

Which battles? The ones about the New York State Theater itself or for Lincoln Center?

The whole thing; well, the Opera House mainly. That was the big money. And I don't know – the Philharmonic [Avery Fisher Hall] too. How that money got raised – it was all nip and tuck at the last minute. And then Robert Moses – the city came into it and gouged out the park there. He was very helpful at condemning all the rest of the needed space. We couldn't have done it without Moses. The planning became infinitely more difficult.

And then poor Wally Harrison. He was our leader, as it were, and he was a lovely man, but not a particularly gifted architect. He had terrible trouble because the space left for him at the Opera site was too narrow. So the monster [the Metropolitan Opera] got longer and longer and longer. It was very hard to plan that at that time, so the ending was that there's no front space. So I had the only one, the only room in the front of the building. That's why the city, as well as other people, use the State Theater for events; you couldn't use the Met or the Philharmonic for anything. But Wally was stuck; he just had this long, narrow box.

Then, of course, there was another very lucky thing for me – that I had a boss like Kirstein, because when theater people start-

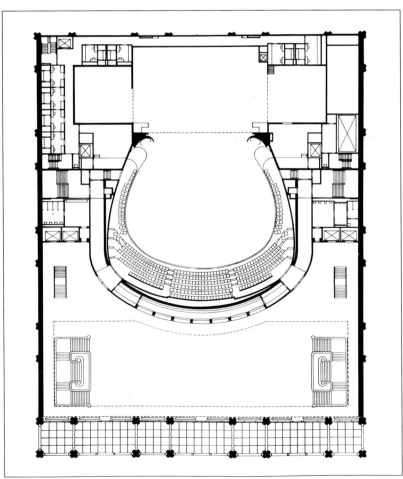

FLOOR PLAN SHOWING FIRST RING

ed to work on the project, they wanted to know, "Where's the backstage?" There isn't any backstage. We were going to have one, and then we sat down one day and said, "Shall we have a backstage or a foyer?" The Met decided to have a backstage. They have stages and stages back there. But Lincoln said, "Well, if we have to pick, I'd rather have the foyer."

Has the lack of a backstage in your building been a problem for the City Opera?

The City Opera complains that that's not the way to do it. The dancers can get along.

We were curious about your relationship with Lincoln Kirstein and also with Nelson Rockefeller. Can you tell us how you all knew one another? You had met Mr. Kirstein at Harvard, right?

Let's go further back. Yes, I had met Lincoln at Harvard, and I approved – he was a rebel who was interested in modern art and

The Met decided to have a backstage. But Lincoln said, "Well, if we have to pick, I'd rather have the foyer."

modern literature and had a little private magazine, the *Hound and Horn*. He was wealthy. The Society of Contemporary Art was his visual side. I didn't know him well at Harvard. But later on we became very close friends. He liked my architecture.

George Balanchine was one of the great artists of our era. I went with Lincoln to Paris to see the opera, to see the ballet. And so we talked about ballet theaters. Lincoln, you see, is a great classicist; he doesn't like what I do now. He only likes the classical. So we have pleasant fights. He has turned against modern art; he doesn't even like Picasso or Matisse anymore, although he was one of their early backers, with Alfred Barr and others at MoMA.

But we were very close. Nelson, of course, had headed the Modern and had headed almost everything, and then he had become head of the state. It was an absolutely ideal combination. And so we weren't touched by all the infighting with Moses or the city or anything like that. I was the luckiest architect in the world, I guess. I didn't know it was happening. I didn't know Nelson was there doing all this, because it appeared like magic, the money for this project. It's not a cheap building.

When I first got this job, there was a discussion by Nelson about whether we could build across the street and get nearer to the park. Nelson wanted a platform over the whole square, so we'd have a private bridge and plaza, leading over and then eventually down into the park.

Why was that not done? It was just too expensive?

Probably. You'd have to buy all these apartment houses and churches and tear them down. Nelson didn't mind; I didn't mind. But we don't have the power to destroy old cities anymore, do we? Not on the upper west side of Manhattan. There was an enormous battle to get that much land. If it hadn't been for Moses, we never would have got it.

Did you work directly with Moses?

No. That was all handled at a wonderfully higher level. But Nelson had a terrible time with Moses. Oh, they fought the whole time. I know, because the World's Fair, for which I also did a building for the state, was happening at the same time, right in the middle of the design for the theater. Nelson told Moses that he wanted the tallest building at the fair. It was Nelson's state, and this private enterprise was taking his land. Nelson thought that the state building should be the tallest building. Moses said, "Absolutely not. We have a height rule here, and I can't do that. What would Great Britain or anybody else say if you, this little state, had the highest building?"

The design was practically finished, you see. So Nelson came in and said, "Philip, how can you make this the tallest building?" Because of Nelson's request, I added the towers to the New York State Pavilion.

Then we didn't have the money to build it. They funded the state pavilion at the last minute in Albany. The legislature worked until six o'clock in the morning and set the clock back, so we got it, $15 million more. And $15 million in those days was a lot more than it is now.

What was on the outside of the theater building at the New York State Pavilion? Didn't you apply artwork by pop artists to the exterior of the structure?

Oh, yes, around one of the buildings. We ran into political trouble there.

Wasn't Andy Warhol's Ten Most Wanted Men *the group of pieces you used?*

Yes. The paintings were his, but the "wanted men" turned out to have mostly Italian names. The governor hit the ceiling.

How do you feel when you're driving out on the Grand Central Parkway and pass the old fairgrounds? Do you get a kick out of seeing the building, or does it disturb you that the area is no longer being used?

I feel very funny. Nothing disturbs me about it – it's a ruin. I like ruins. It just has those cables – no roof. It's a folly now. It's rather nice.

Begun in 1966 and finished in 1973, the Boston Public Library addition was the first project that Johnson built with his longtime associate John Burgee. Johnson and Burgee had their work cut out for them: the commission required adding to one of the most accomplished buildings of the nineteenth-century architectural masters McKim, Mead and White.

The Library Committee rejected Johnson's original design for an obviously classical building with large bulging columns that looked like they belonged in an armory. Johnson then turned to a new, simpler design. The large court within the building is a dramatic and elegant space flanked by stairs of pink granite. There is no question that this space did not arrive out of any sort of functionalist solution. And for this, Johnson was taken to task by critics. Johnson refuses to label the building as postmodern or modern. Instead, he says, it is on the "cusp."

In the end, the library addition met with mixed reviews. Some critics lambasted Johnson for mimicking McKim's building too closely in its detail – the sign of a "bad" modern building. Others found the building simply "too modern." Nevertheless, now over 20 years since the addition's completion, Johnson's classical design has withstood the test of time.

We ran across some criticisms of the Boston Public Library addition that in effect said, "The McKim, Mead and White building is such a masterpiece, how can you really mimic it?" But wasn't McKim mimicking Pierre-François Henri Labrouste?

McKim's was Italian Labrouste. I don't see anything wrong with that. But I didn't mimic. That's exactly what I didn't do, you see. And that was why Henry-Russell Hitchcock's complaint was the opposite. He said, "Well, your building's all right, Philip, but what did you do with the scale?"

The contextualism isn't complete.

Yes, incomplete. I elbowed the scale entirely out. So I did insult the original in a way. I should have kept the scale and nothing else, that is, the scale on the fenestration.

If you were building it today, would you feel compelled to use the same forms and scale of the older building?

Well, I'd be more like McKim, just run the same arcades along the sides.

You would do that?

Well, I wouldn't do it at all. But at the time, I think that was the right kind of compromise. I was doing a modern building. A span

was a 60-foot span – that's the way it's easy to build nowadays. So I thought, we'll start with that and then go backward.

The opposing criticism was that your addition didn't go far enough, that it didn't copy the original's details all the way.

My principle was that the cornice line is sacred; the material is sacred. I used the same quarry McKim had used, and I didn't dare go higher or lower. I thought, it's impossible to do that now. We have to do modern scale. So I built a modern building. And it is "out of keeping," that's right. But I don't see anything wrong with that as long as it doesn't insult McKim.

We looked at the building and thought that if you had done it ten years ago, you might have done something representational with those finials and the other decorative details on the old building. Is that on the mark?

No, it never crossed my mind to pick up the details in any way. I'm a modern architect. And I was very respectful of the material and the cornices.

But if it were 1983, right after the AT&T Building was built, what might you have done?

Well, I never really went back and thought of it that way.

We were fascinated with the back of the McKim building where you've made the connection to the McKim building, which itself becomes less and less articulated as it gets closer to your building. We assumed McKim designed it that way because this part of the

My principle was that the cornice line is sacred; the material is sacred. I used the same quarry McKim had used.

building is farther away from Copley Square and therefore not in view as much.

Yes, well, McKim didn't really care about that back section of the building.

We noticed that your building blends in rather nicely with it. Were you paying close attention to that?

Very close attention, yes. I wondered what he was suggesting. Well, he turned the corner in a little bit, see, so I let him – I freed up the corner, on purpose.

In the original model for the addition, there were these curious columns. What made you decide to delete the engaged columns from the final plan?

The board. They hated it. It looked too much like an armory. You know, the medieval feel. My first design was much more medieval, you see.

The exterior of the original design, with the half-moon or eyebrow windows and the original fat, rounded columns, had an almost Frank Furness quality.

Oh, good. You are much better critics than the ones we had in those days.

It also has the repetition of the little punched, rectangular windows that appear in the old building.

And they reduce that big, broad scale, don't they?

John Doherty, who was a project manager for cost control, told us, "We think the building is superb; it works perfectly. I would change nothing." He said that the critics at the time and almost to this day complained about the atrium: "What a waste of space." He said if he had not built that atrium, the building would have been full within six months anyway. And now 20 years later, the library still has this elegant space.

Build elegant space that people can't change into carrels or something else. But really, the atrium is not an atrium; it's the center of nine squares. It's the idea of communication, like McKim's. My atrium isn't as nice as his. Well, his is a court. Mine isn't a court or even an atrium; it's too small. It's a stairwell. But it's still an orientation point. From each side of all the floors, you can check in. In no other library these days can you get anywhere from anywhere. You just get lost totally.

It was the same problem in New York at the NYU Library, which everyone hated because of all that space at the center. Well, we wanted some more space for books and we wanted to be able to get access. The BPL is perfectly all right, but the new Columbia library, you can't find your way around there.

You also used a nine-square plan at Dumbarton Oaks, which you were doing at about the same time. Was there any connection between these two works?

No, I never even thought of nine square. Those kinds of things are subconscious.

Who were you working with? To whom did you report?

I worked with the librarian who was a wonderful man, Philip McNiff. He's still around, retired. But it was really the board. They were so busy and their minds were on other things. There was just one unpleasant meeting. Well, at that meeting, the li-

ELEVATION OF JOHNSON'S FIRST PROPOSAL FOR BPL ADDITION

brary was about to fire me, or it would have, if I hadn't become a little easier to work with. They said, "We don't think that's a very good design." I said, "Well, I don't know quite what you're talking about, but I think I do." I went back and changed it all. No, I had a very sympathetic librarian.

The materials you used seem so elegant. Was the addition very expensive to build?

Yes, but the City of Boston, Mayor Kevin White, was a very good backer.

The library actually came in under budget and was finished six months ahead of time. Wasn't there another firm that worked on the building as well?

A local firm. The project was so difficult that John Burgee practically relocated to Boston to work on it. It's the first job that has his name on it as my partner, because he had to do practically all the details.

Is his "signature" on the building anywhere?

Nothing to show, because the library was already designed before he came.

He was the one that got it built; it really was bogged down. I'm not very good at that part of it. Things get awfully tangled up on a job this big, you know. He'd go out and spend days there straightening them out. He was wonderful.

Did you have any input on how the shelving and other interior details and furniture were placed?

Of course, but it was clear that it wasn't going to be final, because uses change and sequences change, unforeseeable things, so I knew my plan was going to go. And it did in fact very soon. We never did get the entrance straight. The requirements for security changed exactly at that moment, and I had none of those details as part of my design.

The entrance area was originally just open?

Yes, you just walked into the public library as it is. The same thing with NYU. I didn't have all that crud.

So did someone else do the designs for the security area, or were you called in to do it?

No, another company did it.

So that's not your design at all?

No, I kept fighting, but I kept losing.

We had heard that those granite slabs in front of the great big plate glass windows on the first floor were designed as a reflection of the times, 1968, 1969, 1970 – student unrest, you know. Is that true?

No, I just didn't see any sense reading a book looking at automobiles. But I wanted windows there.

So it's almost a secluded garden hidden behind the slabs?

Yes. I wanted this "in" and "out" feeling, you see. In the original design there were no windows. That's a bit grim. The original

In the original design there were no windows. The original design *does* look like an armory, like the one on Columbus Avenue in Boston.

design *does* look like an armory, like the one on Columbus Avenue in Boston. It's very medieval. It looks like it should have been brick, doesn't it? That dark red brick used in armories in the 1880s and 1890s.

In this final design, did you have the hidden gardens on the top window story?

Yes, planting boxes. Well, it would have been nice on the outside too, similar to what we did at The Museum of Modern Art. There our landscape architect, Bob Zion, planted ivy that hangs down the building.

You also planned for ivy to cascade from the top in a Marshall Field building facade in Dallas, Texas. Why didn't you try creating similar hidden gardens in the Neiman Marcus building in San Francisco?

You can't dictate scenes like that. In the Neiman Marcus building, the whole point was to walk into a grand entrance. But their idea was when the customer comes through an entrance, they sell; as soon as you get into the building, you have got to be handed something to be paid for.

But I said to them, "Look, this is where the customer comes in. You can start the sales just beyond this point. The shoppers can't miss it." But no, they insisted that they had to be right in the front of the vestibule with merchandise.

Do you find that designing a commercial environment is less satisfying than, say, a library that is a monument?

Yes. Churches are the best.

We heard that when the BPL's stairway was finished, you arrived early one morning in a coat that looked like a black cape. You walked up the stairs and said, "I've always wanted to do this."

That's perfectly true. They were the first grand stairs I got to do.

Are these your best stairs?

Well, the State Theater at Lincoln Center, of course, is the best of my monumental stairs. In Boston, I was still using straight lines

The marble staircase or a granite stairway is the greatest thing in architecture.

like I did at the Four Seasons restaurant in the Seagram Building. The marble staircase or a granite stairway is the greatest thing in architecture, and they're forbidden now for any purpose. I put that great staircase in the corporate offices at AT&T, and there's never been anybody on it, because it's only for two floors. People go in through the elevator instead.

But the stairs act as a dramatic device.

Sure. It's a device – a magnificent one – when used well. You couldn't help but use the staircase in Turin, the one at the great Palazzo Madama that goes up and up and up and up. Staircases are a baroque invention, of course. The Renaissance, for example, had no great stairs.

In Renaissance churches, sometimes you find small stairs going up to the front entrance.

Oh, at the front doorsteps, but they never had steps in their palaces. Look at the Fogg Museum at Harvard, for instance. It's all hidden. They're terrible stairs.

You're hot and tired by the time you walk up to the third floor.

Not only that, but you get bored, and you get in a non-picture-looking mood by going up there. At this library your feeling as you go up is that there must be something important up there.

It's like town halls, justice buildings in the nineteenth century, especially in old courthouses. They're just marvelous that way. I mean, you feel the majesty of the law, you get scared to death. You get that, "Gee, are they going to arrest me too?" sort of feeling. But you see, those feelings for doing architecture with regard for the processional are not considered anymore, ever since Gropius

said, "Does it work? Is it cheap?" Look at that graduate dorm that he did at Harvard!

When we went to the BPL addition, we noticed that a lot of people were using the stairs.

There? I can't believe it.

Yes, they were walking. We also took the elevator and noticed that the cabs were like the ones you had used at the New York State Theater and at MoMA – with that textured metal, almost like a metal watch wristband.

Yes, it's woven. That material got so expensive, but that's what I wanted. I don't remember where the elevators are hidden, but they're meant to be hard to find; that way you're compelled to take the stairs.

They're all the way in the back.

That's where they are at the State Theater.

But they really do use those stairs, and they have a processional feeling like the Widener Library steps at Harvard.

But that's outdoors, at Widener, and it's too long. Like the stair I built in The Museum of Modern Art garden. It's gone now. It was enormous. It didn't go anywhere, see. It was trouble. After seeing three or four pieces of sculpture, why should I climb that stairs to

I don't remember where the elevators are, but they're meant to be hard to find; that way you have to take the stairs.

see one more piece of sculpture? Stairs to nowhere. That was not a very good idea. They have to take you somewhere.

Unless you're Morris Lapidus.

His stuff is pretty grand. But that's why I always liked Morris. I was the only modern architect who liked him, so he and I got to be good friends.

I did the stairs in the museum, and you got tired at the top, because the risers' tread was on the courtyard: 4-inch height and 16-inch depth. Well, that's fine for a few steps, but 4 and 16 multiplied by enough to get up a floor is too shallow. You get much less tired by taking a 6 and 12. Fewer steps and higher. Stairs are very, very tricky. What I didn't like about the processional in the

BPL addition was that the corners were too sharp. That's what I like about the State Theater.

It's very smooth.

Well, it deliberately curved at the turns. But I thought the mood here at the BPL wasn't curves. As a matter of fact, that

The classicists said, "It's not enough like the library." The modernists said, "It isn't modern." You know who liked it? Ada Louise Huxtable.

doesn't fit very well at the State Theater either, but I wanted it. I tried to work stairs into the AT&T Building, but there was just no way to do it on the ground floor.

In the BPL's atrium, or stairway, the corners appear to act like separate pavilions.

They are. I used that all over, little square pavilions. That makes the basic rhythm of the plan.

Was the lighting done to your specifications?

Yes, I had a lighting consultant but I don't think that the lighting is quite adequate. I would work on the contrast between the light in the court and the other light – those things we know more about now.

How did you go about deciding to use the exact same granite as the original? We had heard that the old Milford quarry was reopened for this job.

It happens all the time. The quarry was reopened; that's just a normal thing. It does sound very dramatic, "reopened the original quarry." They weren't selling any stone at that time. It's not hard to reopen.

Could you also tell us about the handling of the stone itself? It's a wide band of granite followed by several slender bands, and it's very beautiful.

It's a little relief from the eternal ashlar – I don't know where it originated, neoclassicism probably.

Do you recall what the public reaction was in Boston?

No, I don't think the public reacted. The students and the critics all reacted: it was horrible! The professors at Harvard – everybody – said it was the worst thing they had seen. They would have said that of anybody.

They said it was horrible?

Oh, sure. The classicists said, "It's not enough like the library." The modernists said, "It isn't modern." You know who liked it? Ada Louise Huxtable of the *New York Times*. So you never know.

We both had the same reaction. We thought that the building had been redone or something, because it feels so fresh. It feels like it was built in the 1980s. The stonework, the serif typeface used for the lettering, resembles what other architects started doing in the mid-1980s. Maybe not as well. However, in terms of the color of the stone and the overall design of the interiors, it certainly feels ahead of its time. Some of the wood looks more of its time, from the 1960s or 1970s. But in general, this project seemed to mark that interesting transition between modern and postmodern.

Yes. I was chosen over I. M. Pei because they thought I was a Renaissance man. I was interested in the history. No other modern architect whom they interviewed would talk about it. But I was very much into it, and I loved McKim. I could talk more learnedly about McKim than others could.

So they thought you would understand the context?

That's right. And I think they were a little disappointed when they saw it.

Mies van der Rohe once said, "God lives in the details." In contrast, Paul Rudolph said, "There are no details." What would Philip Johnson of the era of the Boston Public Library addition have to say about details?

I would have agreed with Paul. You see, what Mies meant by details and what Paul meant are two different things. Mies meant, for instance, the joining of this slab to that or the return from here to there or the actual form of the thing that holds the glass. And that I did pay attention to. But what Paul meant was that there should be no ornament.

If you were forced to cast this building as either modern or postmodern, how would you respond?

It's postmodern, but it's certainly . . .

Right on the cusp.

Yes, it's right on the cusp, that's the word, right. I think that's why nobody likes it. Funny, the nineteenth-century armory reference is perfectly clear in the first design.

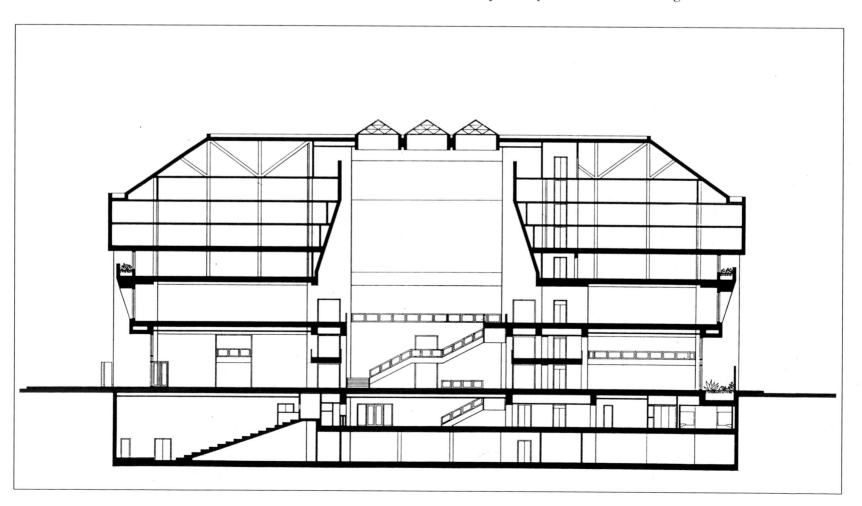

SECTION SHOWING OPEN STACKS AND CENTRAL COURT

It's interesting that you say it's a cusp building, because in fact the Boston Public Library News of 1967 says: "In the case of the new addition, the result has been an inauguration of a completely new style, one which, it is hoped, will prove to be a milestone in architectural history."

Well, maybe it is the beginning of postmodern.

Philip McNiff described the working relationship with you as almost like a marriage. He said that the two of you were of the same frame of mind.

It was unbelievable how well we worked together. McNiff saw the point in what I was doing. He didn't talk about wasted space. Today's librarians!

I know how they couldn't stand me down at NYU. But the president of the university backed me. They said, "My God, what do you think you're doing? All that space. We don't need this open space here." Well I thought they did. My idea of functionalism did not agree with theirs.

But here at the Boston Public Library we had no such problem. See, it came to us by way of a board thoroughly aware of history and wanting a historical addition and my wanting a modern one. And what you see now is the end result. This is the postmodernism that I still approve of in a way. We twist it enough so that we have to ask, "Is it a modern building?" I don't know. It doesn't fit; it's on the cusp. Later, postmodernism became more of what Robert Stern does, more applied or derived. Correctness of the entasis and all that.

Does that bother you, this idea of exactness?

Oh, yes, because it's only what you do with the thing that makes it interesting. My sin, of course, was the Ledoux Building

It was unbelievable how well we worked together. McNiff saw the point in what I was doing. He didn't talk about wasted space.

in Houston [the University of Houston School of Architecture. That's when I really became a postmodernist. And of course, I think it is the best building on campus, and that went to my head, you see.

But what turned me off postmodernism was the quality of the details. What McKim did so beautifully here in the Boston Public Library was to improve on Labrouste and learn something from Alberti's church in Rimini. But McKim understood proportions, and his depth and sequence are very good.

It's the details. I couldn't even do it. On the inside of AT&T for instance. My columns there are perfectly all right on their own. But the way these things fit is just all wrong. I said to myself, "Well, then, why do I work it that way? Why don't I work with a thing where I have a consistency within my own world?"

It's so interesting what you say about the McKim building, because

This is the postmodernism that I still approve of in a way. We twist it enough so that we have to ask, "Is it a modern building?" I don't know.

it really is an Italian reading of Labrouste. In some respects, Labrouste was taking a very modern approach.

He *was* being modern.

And McKim was being more revisionist?

Postrevisionist. Postmodern or revisionist? It really depends on this: Is the architect any good? When Schinkel did Gothic, did he do it better than he did something else? Well, you see, it didn't make any difference what style he picked. He was a great architect. So it's who does it, not what.

Best, of course, was probably Sir John Soane. He's better than Schinkel in his working of classical detail, because he'd warp it enough to make it thrilling. McKim didn't do it very often, just here at the BPL and in the University Club.

That McKim building though, in a way, has a connection to some of your buildings. He too was a Renaissance man, who was educated in a beaux-arts tradition and who also included contemporary art pieces in his building.

He certainly did. But it was contemporary to think in those terms, you see. And it was in Henry Hobson Richardson's time, as well.

Obviously you like McKim. Are there other American architects from the nineteenth century of whom you're particularly fond?

Well, Richardson, of course, is one of my favorite architects. There's a man who understood Romanesque, but yet there's nothing Romanesque about his Quincy Library, for instance. Nevertheless, his work is recognizably Romanesque. Richardsonian Romanesque. Yes, he created his own style. His own thing.

Breaking the Mold

Crystal Cathedral, Garden Grove Community Church
Garden Grove, California
1977-1980

AT&T Corporate Headquarters
New York, New York
1979-1984

Johnson insists that he loves religious buildings because they really allow the architect to be expressive. In the Crystal Cathedral, as it is popularly known, Johnson created a church like no other for a congregation unlike the rest. His client, Dr. Robert Schuller, the dynamic head of the Garden Grove Community Church, televises his services from one of the best-known ministries worldwide.

The program here was to create a church that would allow the sun to reach the California-based congregation. Johnson used glass, thousands of panes of the stuff, within an intricate web of metal tubing in the form of a distorted star, which he claims comes from German expressionism. The most extraordinary feature of the church, and Johnson's favorite, is the set of doors behind the pulpit, which can be opened electronically so that congregants outside in cars can observe the service. These Johnson fondly refers to as the "Cape Canaveral" doors. At 90-feet tall, they do look like they could house a product of NASA.

The Crystal Cathedral is not only a house of worship. It is a building used for performances with religious themes. Easter and Christmas spectaculars are staged within the church to sold-out houses. Johnson took note of this when he created the form of the church, which is wider than it is long. This design brings more of the congregants closer to the pulpit than more traditional long-naved churches.

Johnson also produced a new spire and chapel for Dr. Schuller in 1990. The free-standing spire looks more like the outline of an expressionist skyscraper than a conventional spire. It is constructed out of polished steel that glistens like glass in the California climate. The original church that the Crystal Cathedral supplanted was designed by Richard Neutra.

How did Dr. Robert Schuller first approach you about the commission for the Crystal Cathedral?

Dr. Schuller walked in the door and I wasn't here, so he spoke to John Burgee. John thought he was looking for work because he asked him, "Can I see you about a job?" John couldn't figure out what this man was doing here, so John maintained an "I don't think there's anything open right now" attitude.

Well, Dr. Schuller was here to give a job. He was not looking for one. Schuller asked John Burgee, "Do you think I would have a good spiritual relationship with Mr. Johnson?" This was before he met me. John Burgee didn't know what to say, so he said, "Yes, I think you would," you know.

So we met. He had seen my name in *Time.* I was one of the architects around. He told me to come see him "to see how the spiritual connection," the chemistry, in other words, would work. It worked fine and I wanted to do the job. I got very religious.

We talked and talked and talked and I designed a church for him. He came east and we sat down and I noticed this dreadful si-

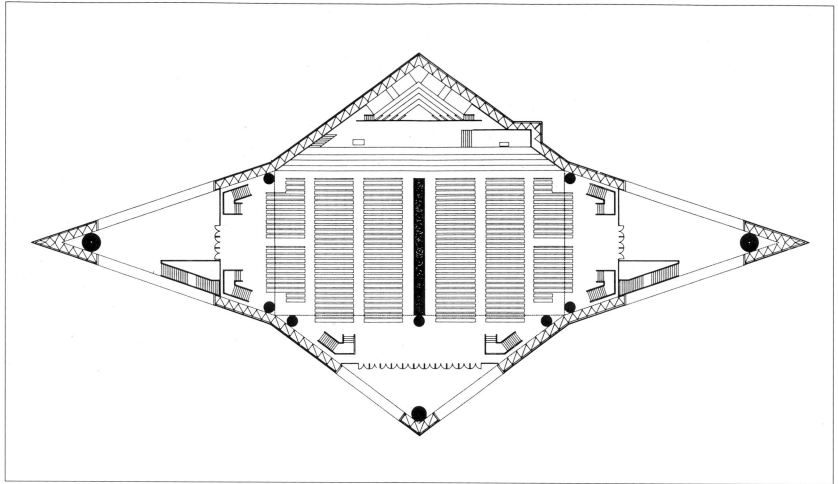

CRYSTAL CATHEDRAL, PLAN

lence. He's not a silent man. Quiet isn't one of his goals. So I said, "Oh God, what have we done?"

What we had done in the first design was keep the sunlight out of the building. I had thought he'd had enough of that. You'd want to go in and get religion – not sun. He said, "Look, this is California, you have to understand. We like to be outdoors, and why not?

It was a little hard to build, but Dr. Schuller rose to the occasion and said, "If you've got to give to God, don't you think it should be expensive?"

I preached outdoors for many years, on top of a truck. I think I want to go on preaching that way."

I realized that we'd gone down the wrong track with that first design. But here we now had an opportunity to make a glass building. He was ecstatic about it.

How did you come up with this particular form – the star – for the plan of the church?

It more or less came from expressionism, I suppose. It's distorted, flattened, the long axis no longer leads to the speaker but cuts across. I wanted people to be all the same distance from the preacher. I don't like long, thin chapels because they don't emphasize the speaker. It would never do for an evangelist's church. In his old church, he had to speak at one end, so it was in revolt against that that I did this distorted star.

The oblong shape, and the broad axis, as opposed to a long, narrow axis typically seen in churches, makes this plan seem essentially baroque, like Bernini's Sant' Andrea in Rome.

Sant' Andrea of course was in my mind.

So the altar really becomes a stage.

Naturally, he liked it when it was all done. It was a little hard to build, but Dr. Schuller rose to the occasion and said, "If you've got to give to God, don't you think it should be expensive?"

Was this commission particularly interesting to you because it was a religious building?

Oh, I'm mad for religious buildings. The only thing that really gives you a kick in the world is a religious building. Buildings like houses should be done by the people who live there. There's

no reason for architects to spend all their energies on houses. If you spend it on religion, then you make monumental space, which gives you a kick. And what's the point of a space unless it gives you a kick? Symphony halls can do that, but even they, for acoustical reasons, want to be boxes. In a religious building you have carte blanche.

We noticed the absence of traditional symbols like the crucifix.

He didn't want it. There's a cross inside on the edge of the stage. I did exactly what Dr. Schuller wanted. Personally, I like cult objects. To me, the cross is one of the great symbols of all

Oh, I'm mad for religious buildings. The only thing that really gives you a kick in the world is a religious building.

time and I make an awful lot of it, whether it's Celtic or something else. But that isn't what he had in mind. It was to be ecumenical. Dr. Schuller, being a very good preacher, knew what he wanted.

Unlike your work in the AT&T Building, here you allowed for a lot of client input. Did you think that you could actually achieve a better building by doing that?

Sure, because when he refused the church design, he was right. Sometimes that happens. The only freedom to design I've really had is in my own house. No trouble having input there. I had input, all right – my own.

Did you handle the interior design of the Crystal Cathedral?

No. I just worked on the architecture. They didn't keep the seats that we had. They took them down because he wanted people to be more comfortable, and I had thought he wanted more people. Originally there were more pews.

And he wanted comfort instead?

Not he, the donors. Things like that. I also lost on the organ. He kept buying organs.

We were struck by the feeling that the entire campus of the Crystal Cathedral was one of ecclesiastical entertainment. There is a gift shop, a snack bar with tables under umbrellas, all in a neatly tailored landscape. Since so much of this existed before your building was planned, how did you negotiate combining your sacred space with Schuller's quasi-commercial spaces?

You get into the spirit of commercial religion. Schuller would have answered that, "How am I going to get along if I'm not appealing to the consumer public?"

I thought God died some time ago, depending on whom you listen to. However, if a Catholic priest came to me to do a church, I'd have no trouble. You accept the premises of the religion that you're working for.

But everything in Dr. Schuller's church is cash-oriented. They sell burial plots of all shapes and sizes. For a little tiny plot in the prime space, you pay a mere $200,000. You can be underneath the beautiful spire for $150,000. If you want to be buried in an urn, that's a lot less. A bargain because it takes up one square foot!

I'm surprised you're surprised. I mean, this is America and television is very expensive.

Are you surprised that the Crystal Cathedral didn't have a greater influence on church architecture as a whole in the United States?

No, I'm not at all surprised. It's very expensive and parishes are notoriously poverty-stricken. But Dr. Schuller's church is not a parish. He is a worldwide force.

What feature of the church excites you the most?

Well, I had a unique opportunity to make the big Cape Canaveral doors and to create a star of glass. That concept of glass

I thought God died some time ago, depending on whom you listen to. However, if a Catholic priest came to me to do a church, I'd have no trouble.

dates back to 1914. But modern techniques gave me a chance to stretch engineering a bit – to actually build it. John Burgee did a wonderful job for us.

Were the Cape Canaveral doors originally intended to give the drive-in worshippers a view?

Yes. But the view has been shifted around because they have moved the parking lot over. Now there's a gigantic television screen mounted outside, so that you can watch what's going on inside from the car.

How long did it take you to produce the design?

A couple of years. No longer than any other.

You mentioned that it was difficult to do the construction. Did you have problems with glass falling out?

No, no. But it's still very hard to wash.

The building is known as the Crystal Cathedral even though it is officially called the Garden Grove Community Church. What do you think about the new name?

Well, if you come from a Catholic background, that isn't helpful in understanding modern religion. It isn't crystal, and it isn't a cathedral.

But it has its own exit sign on the highway.

It's a tourist trap.

Can you tell us how you designed the new tower? Was it part of the original design?

No, it is entirely different. I always wanted to do religious things anyhow. So when Dr. Schuller came to me about the tower, I didn't charge him for the project. My first question was, "What material are you going to use for it?" You couldn't build a tower in glass, you see. So I built a Gothic tower, a Gothic spire in polished stainless steel.

How much time did he give you to produce it?

Well, he really didn't give me any time. He simply said, "Give me a tower."

Do you have a favorite aspect of the cathedral?

The important feature is the prow, I think. The doors should be closed for that view, of course.

Were you responsible for any of the landscape designs?

None. I think that Schuller wanted to keep the landscaping for himself. It is like everybody knows about landscaping, like clothes. When he got me to do the church, I wanted to do the landscaping then too.

Do you often not anticipate all the building's effects when you design something?

Oh, of course. Usually some of the best things I could never anticipate. That 90-foot door – Cape Canaveral or not – it's a technical wonder to open that big door. What's so exciting is to watch a door of that size slowly open.

The building that put Johnson back at the forefront of American architectural discussion is the AT&T Building, which has become an icon of postmodernism. What makes this building so special is that it was designed at a time when corporate headquarters were indisputably being built on the model of the sleek glass and metal Seagram Building. Johnson rejected all that was then conventional wisdom in corporate architecture by proposing to build a stone-clad structure in pink granite with bronze details, amid a veritable sea of marble.

The client, AT&T chairman John DeButts, was a "one-man democracy" and a perfectly fabulous client who allowed Johnson to realize a new vision of corporate fantasy. A monument for a monumental company, the building's fortunes have been tied to those of AT&T, who leased the office tower to Sony Music Entertainment, Inc., in 1991. Sony has since redone the lobbies and base, changing the pedestrian experience of the building drastically by enclosing the once-cavernous cathedral-like base into a shopping arcade.

Johnson looked back towards the great towers of the 1920s for inspiration with AT&T. Its signature top is not meant to be Chippendale, as Johnson tells it. But what of it? Johnson's attention to the base and the interiors is sometimes lost in the discussion, due to the distinctive broken pediment that caps the building. The interiors are at once sumptuous and coolly corporate. Now changed by the new owners, the original style of the interiors is captured only in photographs. The sky lobby was an imperial box of white Carrara marble, floor to ceiling. The main entrance was a vaguely Romanesque setting for a large gold statue that symbolized AT&T. In its conception, the AT&T Building was truly a temple to commerce, albeit not one universally worshiped.

Tell us how you first got the commission. Were you contacted by John DeButts, the chairman of AT&T?

Oh, no. He didn't know one architect from another. It was the best experience I've ever had. We'd never done a big building from one of my ideas. We were on a list of 24 architects the search committee was looking at. The chance of a partnership like ours getting the job, a one-man shop against all those other firms – so we didn't answer it. Why bother to answer all these things that come in? It usually costs $100,000 to $200,000 to compete for these jobs and we didn't have it, so we knew we weren't in that league. We put it aside. About two months later, we got a call from somebody down there who said, "You're the only architect that hasn't answered yet, when can we come around?" And I said, "Okay, come next Wednesday."

So they came – a very, very nice committee. I showed them a blank office – we didn't have any boards, we didn't have any sheets, we didn't have a spiel, we didn't have a video or a lot of designs for a telephone company building. You normally make the designs and work on them for weeks. Well, we hadn't. So we said, "What can we do for you? Sure, we do buildings." They were flabbergasted because they'd seen 23 long, boring expositions. We had no idea about that. We thought ours was the only one.

They were so impressed.

Was Mr. DeButts at the meeting?

Oh, no, he didn't go around looking. They were so impressed by the "aw, shucks" attitude that they put us on the list. Then we interviewed again, including Mr. DeButts.

Did you bring a design to the interview?

No, we don't do that. You're not supposed to anyhow. I told them it should be the most important job I've ever done and will ever do.

Did you know at the time that this building would turn out to be an icon for both postmodernism and for your office? Did you say to yourself, "I want this to be more significant than anything I've done before?"

I got the job, dear. Well, you see a budget like AT&T's – it helps a lot. The nature of the client was so marvelous, his being the chairman. DeButts said to me, "Now, look, I don't want just another building. We'd like to make the next step in tall building architecture since the Seagram Building – just go to it." We thought we'd use pink stone, and he was overwhelmed with delight, so we did it, that's all.

Prior to getting the commission, did you want to build a tall building of that nature, all in stone, as opposed to what you had done in Houston with the Pennzoil towers?

Oh, naturally, postmodernism was very much in the air. Bob Stern used the word first, and I went along with it out of sheer fatigue with the International Style. So the reaction at AT&T was that the building was to be people-friendly. I must have been out of my mind, but it was understandable and was received well. Well, it was and wasn't. You can't do a prominent building like that without being more hated than loved.

Did you quote specific historic buildings?

I was looking at early Romanesque, of course. I don't think I got it looking at specific buildings or books. I looked at McKim.

Is the AT&T your favorite postmodern work?

No, for different reasons, the PPG Building is.

You were experimenting with historical references for years before the AT&T Building, in structures like the Boston Public Library addition or more directly in the Dade County Cultural Center, which looks as if it could be from 1927 instead of 1977. Why the fuss over AT&T by the public? It seems rather tame now.

It surprised me too. The only really bad response was *New York* magazine. They made a list of the buildings New Yorkers love to hate, and they ranked AT&T with that one at Columbus Circle [by Edward Durell Stone]. But most people come up to me when I walk by there and say, "Thank you for this great building."

Some critics dismissed the AT&T building outright during the design stage for the broken pediment at the top.

Ada Louise Huxtable hated it. She's still a modernist.

Was she the one who said that you turned it into a joke with one stroke of a pen?

I didn't know that! That's a good phrase. It ought to be from her, if it isn't.

How did you come up with that form?

Models and experiments. I'd always been impressed by the period of Hadrian and Asia Minor – it's all much more interesting

than Greece. But it was a normal thing to break the pediment somehow, though it is so much against the canons. I had a classicist working for me at the time who said, "You can't do that! You have to put back the molding." That was fun and games for us. And then DeButts ran into so much trouble with his people because of what we were doing with the pediment. He asked me, "Is that the only thing we can do at the top?" And I said, "Oh, no, heavens no." So we came down the next week with a lot of cardboard tops for him to look at. Our first one was still the best.

The character of the former AT&T Building is being altered by its new tenants, Sony Music. Did Sony approach you concerning the changes?

I was told, but not asked. I was only asked about closing in the plaza. That's what they were interested in because they knew that would have an impact on the public, and they were afraid of legal matters – our agreement with the city.

Because of the zoning changes?

Yes, so I testified for them downtown because I am for the changes. The space was basically tailored to AT&T – it is an imperial space. Madison Avenue is a shopping street, not an imperial street. AT&T didn't want lingerie stores in the lobby. They said, "Make it the front door into our empire. Let's make it so you'll be impressed when you go by."

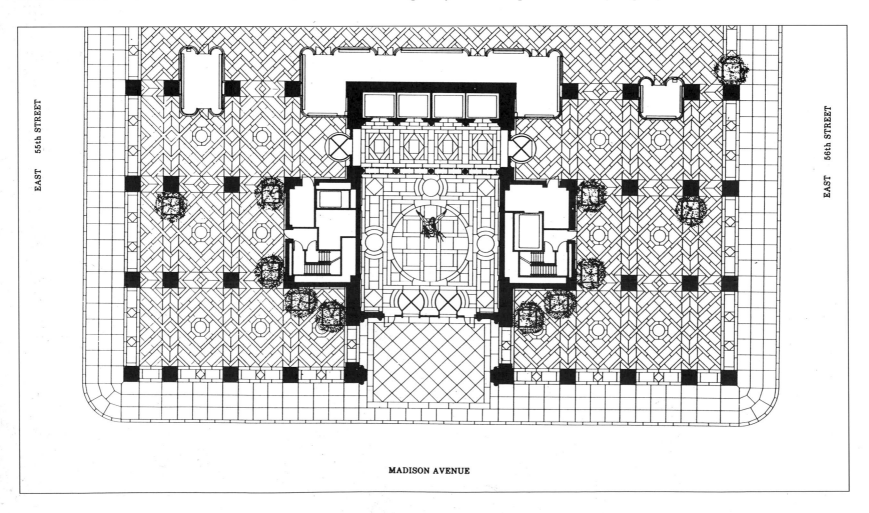

AT&T BUILDING REAR SHOPPING ARCADE

Originally, if AT&T had not wanted as imperial an image, would you have suggested enclosing the atrium?

No, at that time, it seemed to me a good urban statement to make a palatial break in the street, much as the Palazzo Massimo on the Corso Vittorio Emanuele in Rome does, turning a slight angle, which is, of course, a better trick than I had done. But I think shopping in the base of a building is quite risky. You can go on shopping once you have passed the base of the AT&T Building, and it doesn't seem to hurt you any. You simply cross the street and you shop on the other side. I thought leaving retail out of the base level wouldn't hurt at all, and in fact it would ensure the presence of AT&T.

Well, that argument fell upon deaf ears with Sony because they want to sell their goods. If they're going to have an executive building they want to be sure that the whole place is selling Sony. I understand that perfectly. Madison was meant to be a shopping street. The city had never liked the monumentality interrupting the passenger foot traffic. So I felt the city would like the new scheme. I liked it too because the old situation was so monumental that the area at the base wasn't used and became cold and unfriendly. The small chairs that were placed there contradicted the monumentality, which I knew they would. Those chairs were a city requirement. But putting seats in doesn't make people sit in them. They were so small and out of scale with the whole thing, it's kind of amusing. But apart from that ironic scale shift, there wasn't much to be amused about. After all, you don't see chairs in Piranesi arcades.

Of course, the IBM Building's court, next door to AT&T, is really user-friendly. The people who used to be called bums enjoy it

AT&T didn't want lingerie stores in the lobby. They said, "Make it the front door into our empire. Let's make it so you'll be impressed when you go by."

too. And why not? They're part of New York, for goodness sake, and they just add to the local color, as far as I'm concerned. I just love that park.

You would have preferred the base to have been an open space with no seating?

Yes. An open, imperial space. They were an imperial company and they thought of themselves that way. Chairman DeButts was a one-man democracy. He wanted to build. Nobody on the board wanted to build a building.

His way of voting was just wonderful. He didn't ask about a secret vote or anything. He simply informed his board, "I know you'd all be for it, gentlemen."

How it got built was that Mr. DeButts wanted it and he lived in New York. Everyone else lived in Basking Ridge, New Jersey. So the Manhattan building was a headquarters, but AT&T never

They were an imperial company and they thought of themselves that way. Chairman DeButts was a one-man democracy.

used it. They had a token force here to show their flag in New York. It was a big tax deduction and all that, but their heart stayed in Basking Ridge. All the offices stayed there. The chairman had two offices, here and there. So the new building was an expensive whim on DeButts's part, and he was very proud of it.

Do you find that most clients do not want input, that they really prefer to leave the architect to provide the service?

That's right. Well, they try to.

Can you tell us about the stair that connects the executive floors? The curve of that staircase reminded us of what you had done at the New York State Theater.

Well, the real reason for the stairs was the monumental connection. You can go back and take the elevator if you want to, but the stairs are the monumental approach to the boardroom and the executive suites. I thought the stairway would give you a sense of connection, which it does. It's a long flight.

When you first walk into the main lobby and look up at the ceiling, you notice the beautiful gold-leaf vaulting. Had you used that many times before?

At the New York State Theater and the pavilion in New Canaan. I like gold ceilings. It seemed right to me.

You often leave your ceilings bare and clean. There are very few lighting fixtures, there's nothing hanging.

Holes for lighting fixtures? If you have to do the lighting, get rid of those holes. Is there any other period of architecture having a lot of holes in the ceiling?

From the 1950s through the 1970s, most modern architecture used cheap materials. We consider the AT&T Building and postmod-

ernism as breaking off with this practice that proclaimed, "Don't be so restrained. It is okay again to use beautiful materials in an elegant, finished manner." What prompted this return to high-quality materials for you and for others?

I just think that if you've got money and you want to make an important statement, you use good material. As Mies van der Rohe did in the Barcelona Pavilion – in one useless pavilion. Mies was looked down on by the moderns in Berlin in the 1920s because he used silk curtains in his houses. That's the way that most people, if you leave them alone, will do it.

John Ruskin, were he alive today, would no doubt chastise you mercilessly.

I'd merely laugh at him, "How puritanical you are."

And you're not puritanical?

I am not. Well, I fight against it, let's say. I suppose I am terribly puritanical.

Was there ever a plan for an AT&T-owned park or plaza across Madison Avenue from the building?

Just in my mind. I told AT&T, "Why don't you buy the block across the street and make a park, then you'd have a monument," and Mr. DeButts smiled – wanly. It is just like the time I did the plaza at the State Theater. It was Nelson Rockefeller's main desire to push the theater all the way to Central Park. That's why we have governors like Rockefeller. You could have stepped from our front plaza across the other plaza and then terrace down to the park. That was Nelson's idea. He was a great patron, but we didn't have the money.

Why is it, do you think, that the average person who generally doesn't reflect about architecture does remember the AT&T Building so vividly?

There are two things that were done intentionally – the enormous columns, and the top – there's no top like that in New York, although it's not as visible as the tops of tall buildings like the Chrysler. It's unique in that when you do catch sight of it, you don't forget it. That's what I told DeButts. I said, "If we don't do something very striking on top, you won't know your building is up there."

If you say "Philip Johnson" to someone who doesn't know much about architecture, the response will be, "Oh yeah, the one with the Chippendale top." Is this a misinterpretation of your work? Are you offended by this characterization?

No. Just spell the name right.

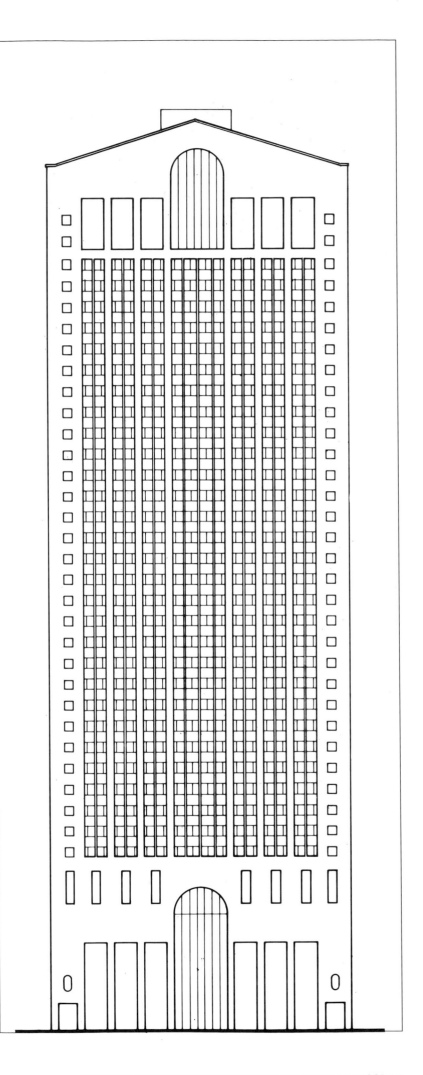

ELEVATIONS SHOWING ALTERNATIVE DESIGNS FOR FACADE AND ROOFLINE

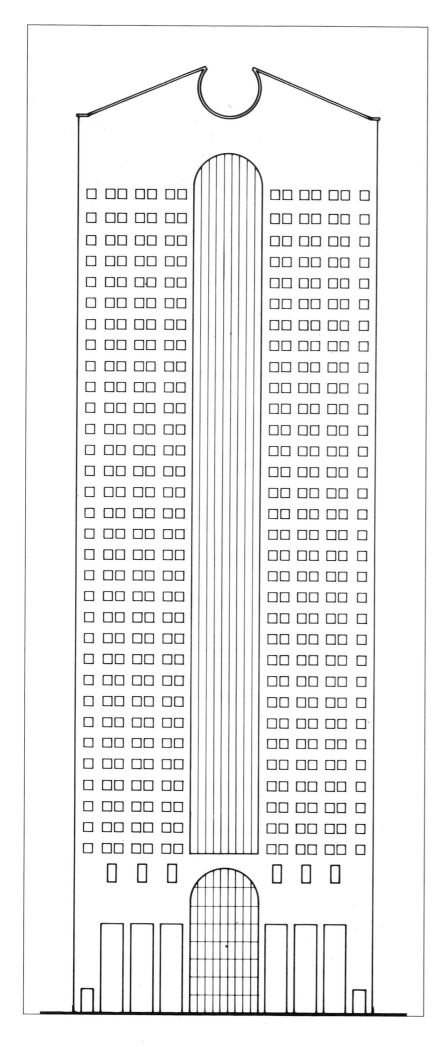
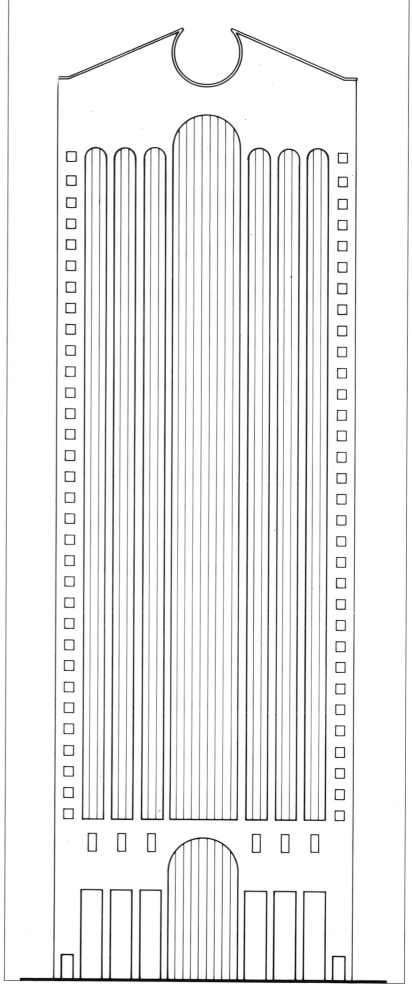

Patrons for Postmodernism

IDS Center
Minneapolis, Minnesota
1968-1973

Pennzoil Place
Houston, Texas
1972-1976

Transco Tower and Park
Houston, Texas
1979-1985

RepublicBank
Houston, Texas
1981-1984

PPG (Pittsburgh Plate Glass)
Pittsburgh, Pennsylvania
1979-1984

Lipstick Building, 53rd at Third
New York, New York
1983-1985

As Johnson and Burgee were overseeing the completion of their 10-story addition to the Boston Public Library, they took on their first commission for a skyscraper. Actually a full square block with four buildings, the IDS Center marked the beginning of a deluge of projects for the firm. Soon Johnson and Burgee would start a fruitful relationship with developer Gerald Hines and by 1987, their high-rises would number about 25. This period would also see corporate America rediscover the art of architecture as well as the notion that buildings could be exploited to convey the image and stature of a commercial enterprise.

Johnson and the public had become bored with the box. At the time, critic Ada Louise Huxtable captured the dissatisfaction with bland modernist utility perfectly. "Today's tall buildings are not stars," she said. "They are impersonally impressive at best, giant nonentities at worst."

In the dramatic and sculptural Pennzoil Place, Johnson changes the equation by experimenting with dramatic non-essential decoration. By the 1980s, with projects for RepublicBank (now NCNB) and AT&T, he is immersed in historicism, his designs as soaring and articulate on American skylines as a Verdi soprano's voice over a full house.

You have talked about how terrific it is to work for a good patron and how that makes for good architecture. Can you tell us about your relationship with your corporate clients and how they participated in the design process, if at all?

That's the most interesting thing from a personal point of view. The relation of patron to architect through the course of history hasn't been investigated enough.

Of course, my relationship with corporate clients begins further back. It begins with Mr. Bronfman, the head of Joseph Seagram and Sons and the patron behind the Seagram Building in Manhattan. He was by far one of the best clients because he was willing to give all the money necessary, whatever the case. "Let's build it in bronze." What a statement to make. He said, "That's a pretty material. Why don't we use that on a door in front of the building?" I nearly fainted. Mies didn't. He merely said, "I think that's a good idea, Mr. Bronfman."

Well, things like that don't happen in this world. I remember Mies and I discussing it afterwards. He said, "Maybe you think that's what architecture is like, Philip," because this was my first building. I said, "Yes!" It isn't, as I have found out.

How did the Seagram commission come about and how did you get involved? It's a Mies van der Rohe building, after all.

Yes, Mies did the building. I was helpful in getting it for him. Phyllis Lambert, Sam Bronfman's daughter, is a very brilliant woman. She was living in Paris, and her father had sent her a picture of the building he was going to build. And she wrote back, "You just can't do that, Daddy. This is much too important a commission to leave to such a bad architect." So her father responded, "Well, you're so smart, you come out and build it." And she said, "I will." And she did. That was the best thing that ever happened, because she was, of course, a divine client for Mies and saw to it that every whim of his was carried out. We rolled through committees as if they were just chaff, you know? She wouldn't stand for any interference from the company.

Now, how we got Mies. Phyllis came in to see me about finding an architect, and I gave her a list. And she went to see them all: Gropius, Saarinen, and Pei. And finally she told me, "I've decided on Mies." Well of course, underneath I'd been pushing Mies all the time. Then Mies picked me, and he came East from Chicago. They made him come here to live while the building was designed. And he didn't like that very much, but he did it. He needed somebody here, so it was helpful for him to have me, of course, because he wasn't registered. They wanted him to take examinations. He said, "No!" Mies felt a bit insecure in New York. He felt that I'd brought him the job and I could be a local man for him, so he made me his partner, which was more than he needed to do. I really wasn't. I didn't work on the building very much.

Did you know Mrs. Lambert prior to that commission?

No, no. She came to Alfred Barr, the head of The Museum of Modern Art, and asked, "What do I do to pick an architect?" And he told her, "Well, Philip's office is down the hall." I didn't have anything to do, strangely enough. I was my own boss. So there were one or two trips I made with her. One to see Mies.

She thought Saarinen was too young. Frank Lloyd Wright was too old-fashioned. That was the attitude toward him in those days, of course, because my sentence was still ringing in everyone's ears, "Frank Lloyd Wright, the greatest architect of the nine-

> There was no budget. They watched, of course, but I mean, the boss had said, "I'd like to build it out of bronze. Wouldn't that be nice?"

teenth century." That wasn't very kind of me, but that's the way we felt then. All this happened before Wright had got his second wind. Anyhow, she picked Mies, and it was a very good move. She followed through; that's the whole thing. There wasn't a decision that she didn't oversee — she overruled her father all the time. There was no budget. They watched, of course, but I mean, the boss had said, "I'd like to build it out of bronze. Wouldn't that be

SEAGRAM BUILDING , NEW YORK

nice?" And Mies answered, "Ja, that would be very nice." You can't imagine anybody saying that today.

Oh, my greatest patron, in a way, was Nelson Rockefeller. Without him I wouldn't have had the New York State Theater or the New York State Pavilion at the 1964 World's Fair in New York City. I was going to do another big thing downtown for him, Battery Park City.

Nelson had the instincts of the greatest patron in the world. He didn't get a chance to carry them out, as Bronfman did, because

> # The clients came to us and said, "We're not satisfied with the facade. Could you please do an outside?" And John, quite rightly, told them that we don't do outsides. We do buildings.

he went into politics. But I think Nelson was an even better patron than he was a politician. He would have accepted anything. He fought Robert Moses to get me to do the New York State Pavilion for the World's Fair.

Did Moses want someone else?

It wasn't that. He didn't want any tall building.

And yet it's the only building that remains.

It's too expensive to take down!

How did your friendship with Nelson Rockefeller develop?

I got to know Nelson through Lincoln Kirstein; it was Lincoln, in fact, more than I, who Nelson really knew and loved. But I got the reflected glory there. And of course, Nelson picked me to do the State Theater – well, Lincoln really did – but this all was done through Nelson. Because Wally Harrison certainly wouldn't have picked me to do the job.

I met Nelson Rockefeller through his mother at The Museum of Modern Art. She told me, "Wait until you meet my son." He was always going around the world and getting educated, or something. He was a kid, only 21 or 22 years old. When he became president of the museum, I got to know him very well. That was a very pleasant friendship indeed. But he was a madman, and Gerald Hines isn't.

Well, Gerald Hines is a businessman.

A businessman, but a businessman with a difference. One with taste. Gerald Hines, of course, is the big patron in my life. And he's a very interesting study.

Prior to your work with Gerald Hines, you did the IDS Tower in Minneapolis. Was that your first tall office building?

Yes. It came about because of John Burgee. He's the one who got me the job. The Dayton family was the patron. Baker, a local man, was the architect. He designed an ordinary half-block skyscraper, but he had placed it on top of a parking structure. The clients came to us and said, "We're not satisfied with the facade. Could you please do us an outside?" And John, quite rightly, told them we don't do outsides. We do buildings.

Then, somehow, we got in it with a young developer there who started to like the cut of our jib. He persuaded the Daytons that only a full block would make any sense and not to build it on top of a garage. If you do that all you'd see when you go by the building is the garage. That's an American habit that I really deplore. So we put the cars down below, and had a chance at a full block. We just turned it inside out in a non-Miesian way. And they loved it.

That job was all about the courage of John Burgee to tell them to go to hell. He told them to fire Baker.

But the client was IDS. How were the Daytons involved?

The Daytons weren't directly financially involved, but they were the big people in town. The head of IDS was the owner of Woolworth's, by descent.

That explains why there is a Woolworth's in the Crystal Court at the IDS Center.

Yes, exactly. We turned the building inside out, which turned out to be the trick. We put a ring of low-rise buildings around the outside of the enormous block, which gave us a chance to have a court inside so that every building faced not only the outside but the central court. That centralized all of the activities of the whole complex. It seemed so obvious to us. Instead of packing a big block, solid and full, we put the buildings around the perimeter, dominated by the skyscraper. So Woolworth's got double exposure. The second-floor walkway was what made that building – it's still not equaled anywhere.

And it's still the center of Minneapolis, despite a lot of subsequent building in that area. Did it come as a surprise to you that you were doing an office tower?

Well, it didn't come as a surprise to John. He practically built it single-handedly. It was on the basis of his work there that I made him a partner.

How did your working relationship with Gerald Hines develop?

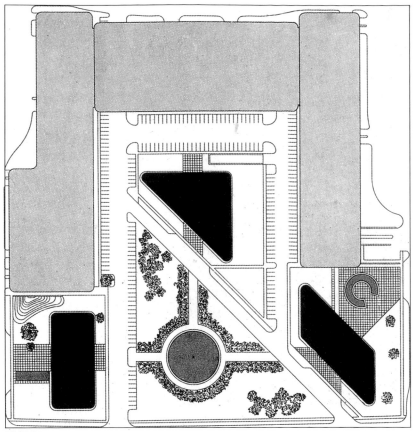

POST OAK CENTRAL

The Hines people came in the damnedest way. It's an interesting story. It was all Mr. Brochstein. He loved me, and I never knew why. He was a great guy. An old-world type. An old cutey pie. He owned some land that Gerald Hines wanted to develop into the Post Oak Central complex. Brochstein told Hines he would have to use his architect. Brochstein had done the woodworking for some of my houses and had always remembered me.

So Brochstein introduced you to Gerald Hines?

He did a little more than introduce us. Brochstein owned the land. To keep Brochstein happy, Gerry came to me. And it worked. Hines was so young in the game. He had never built a big

> # Sklar's wonderful. He's very good at dollars and cents. He has a good builder, John Harris. They're all watchers of pennies.

building. He had done some small office buildings that dot Westheimer, a major thoroughfare in Houston. You couldn't tell them from anyone else's.

But Hines was determined to be different. He didn't know much about real estate back then, because we designed for the project one building for the whole 900-foot length of the property. You couldn't parcel it that way. So we had to take the whole thing over in smaller parcels, and enlarge it as they sold. Of course, it turned out to be an entirely different project.

How much input did Gerald Hines, or his associates, want to have in terms of the design?

Hines developed a good core of people like Louis Sklar, his partner. Sklar's wonderful. He's very good at dollars and cents. He has a good builder, John Harris. They're all watchers of pennies. That's fine, as long as Gerry's there to make sure the projects are interesting.

I've got another story about a client – the Hugh Liedtke story. He was the patron of Pennzoil Place and the company's chairman. He was a cranky old individual. We couldn't get to see him in person except with Gerry. Finally, we went up to see him with Gerry and he told us what he wanted. He wanted a top on a building. He wanted a building with character that would stand out from the undecorated glass boxes around town. So we did a design for Pennzoil Place as it stands there now, with the parrot's beak twist at the top, which intrigues passersby so much.

Liedtke wanted something with a top to it, so I designed a building with a fascinating top. That was my first destruction of Miesian clarity – just for fun, just to do something like that. And Gerry liked it. And Hugh Liedtke thought it was marvelous because it was different from any other building in Houston. But then, Gerry started counting the dollars, and he realized that wasn't the cheapest way to finish the top of that building. So he wrote and made pro formas and said that if we'd agree to take the tops off Pennzoil, he'd build it. He told us to make a model of the revised design.

So we did and took the model with us to the next meeting with Liedtke. Now we had both models. Liedtke exploded, because he felt that we'd lost all of the flavor of the building, because anybody can build a building with a flat top.

I mean, Liedtke can be very irascible. He was really furious when we came back to him with the redesign. He said, "I told you I liked the building. Now you bring me this?" Gerry had made us cut the tops off. He had told us, "You boys cut the tops off and I'll build the building." We were too cowardly to say no. So we did it without the top and took it up to the great man, Liedtke. He turned on Gerry and told him, "Look, I told you I like this building. I do not like a building without a top on it. You cut the darned building off and you expect me to build it? Well, get out of the office!" Gerry doesn't remember it this way, but that's exactly the way it was. And Gerry doesn't remember telling us to take the top off it and he'd build it. But that's where Gerry didn't quite have the courage of his faith.

What pleased Gerry in the end was what he later found out. He had said you could never rent a room that went up at 45 degrees.

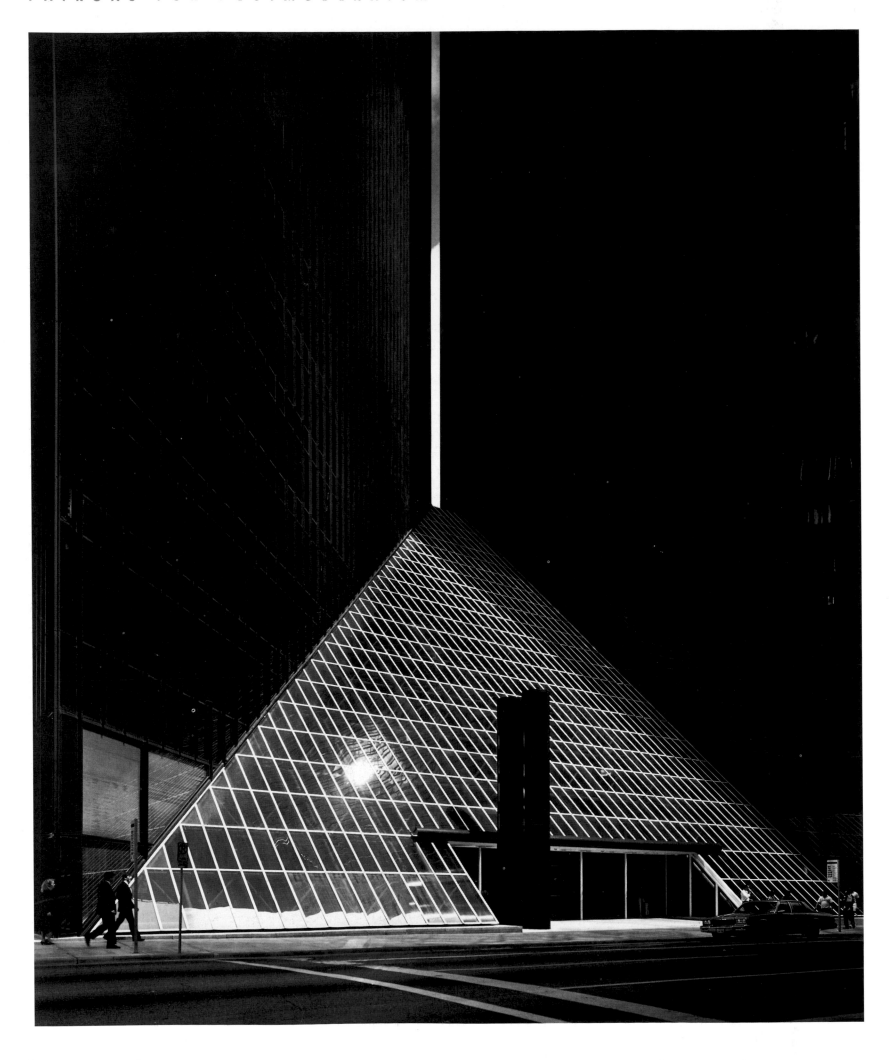

PENNZOIL PLACE ENTRANCE AT COURTYARD

PENNZOIL PLACE COURTYARD INTERIOR

Imagine sitting in a room if it came up at 45 degrees? What he didn't realize – we didn't either, let's face it – was that the strange rooms at the top would rent at much higher prices than the rooms below because they're so special. But Gerry found that out and is

What he didn't realize was that the strange rooms at the top, because they're so special, would rent at much higher prices than the rooms below.

now absolutely delighted, naturally. Now if you buy some of the nice space up in the slant, you have to buy some square footage below. It comes as a package. You can't get just the cream. We've used that story ever since to tell developers that if they create the difference that *makes* the difference they'd be better off. Gerry's always made that point, the point of difference. How can you make this more attractive than the other building? If it costs money, isn't that good money to spend? But it's a very unusual attitude for developers.

In Pennzoil, the two buildings seem to be pulled apart from each other just enough to separate them but close enough to keep the sculptural quality of the composition. How did you decide how far to pull those apart?

Half a bay. Ten feet. I didn't have any great idea about that.

You didn't try anything else?

I should say we did. Because even we knew that was the main point of the building, that slight crack. That's what stops traffic when you're on the freeway.

It seemed very similar to the Lake Shore Drive Apartments of Mies van der Rohe.

It is not. Not at all. Mies wouldn't have done what we did. This was our first break away from Mies to make a shaped geometric form. Others began to do similar things after Pennzoil, like that very popular building of Harry Cobb's in Dallas. That looks like Pennzoil in a way.

What do you like best about Pennzoil Place?

The shape. It was built when I was still modern, but it has an interesting shape. I wrote an article, "The Shape of the Office Building," that discusses that very point. That top is the only

chance I had to do something with these otherwise pretty bland boxes. Mies did it by giving away half the site to a plaza. And of course, today you never do that. What you can do is try to shape the box and do funny things. By the time I was working on RepublicBank, I was fully into my historical period.

How did the Transco project develop?

Jack Bowen of Transco was very interested in glory. He was the head of a large company, and he was interested in art. In fact, he turned one of the lobbies in the Transco Tower into an art gallery. Gerry Hines thought that the suburban area now known as the Galleria district was the beginning of a new, great commercial development. Thank God the real estate bust came – and it came just in time – otherwise the Transco Tower would be surrounded by other tall buildings.

So you like it to stand by itself?

Darn right. I like it alone. I don't want any other buildings around it. Gerald Hines was going to build another building right there. He thought it was wonderful land for development. I said, "Gerry, it is not! It is right in your front door. Why don't you just tell Transco to develop that as a park."

It's about a three-acre park on very valuable land. How did you convince the Hines people to allow it?

It was Transco's decision. Well, Gerry's thinking was that we'll all make money on this eventually, but in the meantime, maybe for the next 20 years, let's do something to attract people to this part of town, to make that area really develop.

And it has developed. In the original park design, wasn't there to be a reflecting pool, as well as the "waterwall" you did build?

Yes, the whole thing was to be water.

Why was this design altered? We heard that there were potential construction and maintenance problems with building a reflecting pool in hot, humid Houston. Were they concerned that you would have an algae problem if the pool were shallow?

The truth was that the land was so unstable that no reflecting pool of that size could have stood up. We all have our own reasons we invented. History is written by the survivors.

Did Jack Bowen express interest in the design?

It's hard to say, because he worked through Gerry. In essence, the clients were told not to put their cotton-picking hands on it. When you think of the cost of that fountain! It was just unbelievable. But Gerry built it anyhow.

TRANSCO TOWER FOUNTAIN

Did you go through any kind of struggle to get Gerald Hines to build that?

No. I told him what a great effect it would be, like Horseshoe Falls at Niagara Falls. To be able to be inside the water! You aren't sure where it's coming from. That intrigued him.

The feature that really makes the Transco Tower stand out, besides not having any other buildings around it, is its very slender proportions. It's a needle-like skyscraper. The rest can tend to be clunky. The secret for that is one of Gerry's brilliant ideas that, if I'd been a developer, I would have said wouldn't work. There we

Gerry Hines knew he had to do something special on Third Avenue in New York, in what is called the "Lipstick" building.

used a sky lobby, which is a developer's word for an elevator exchange. An elevator shaft takes up a lot of dead space. In an ordinary building, you have an elevator shaft for each part of the building: the low-rise, the mid-rise, and the high-rise. But by taking the high-rise shaft and putting it on the top of the low-rise shaft, you save space. The only way you can do that is to have a cross-over floor halfway or two-thirds of the way up. You feed up and down from that cross-over. That sometimes results in having to go up higher than you want to and then going down a few floors to reach a destination, which is strange. But if you can combine your elevators, you get more rental square footage for much less cost. For Gerald Hines, it was cost figuring; for us architects, it was "L over R" [length over radius], or the "slenderness ratio," that made a tall, thin needle instead of a clunky building.

It's a strange idea to build something that tall when you've got that much land around it.

That's Gerry. He and Bowen both wanted the building to end all buildings. And somehow, they can always find the money when they get that desire strong enough. It's so funny. Because otherwise there are many excuses.

Why is it that so many developers don't seem to have that desire?

A lot of people don't have that because they are just after money. None of these boys whom I talk about as patrons are just after money. Gerry thinks he is. But he just plain isn't. Because when he wants to do something like Transco he does.

Would you say that a good architectural patron is not only a businessperson but someone who really loves art?

Someone who really loves art in their particular way. And they're all different. Nelson liked art with a capital "A." I mean, he bought Picassos. Gerry isn't that kind of man. His appreciation is different. He has a special feel for what he wants. He looks for a point of difference that will stand out.

For example, Gerry knew he had to do something special on Third Avenue in New York, in what is called the "Lipstick" building. He couldn't do a regular office tower, because we didn't have

The hard thing to learn – and Gerry was the first to learn it – is that when you build a better building, you'll get better rent.

"location, location, location." This was Third Avenue, not Park. Gerald Hines had no trouble with his tower opposite The Museum of Modern Art. That was location. But over here, in the boondocks? Should you even spend any money on it? Well, yes, building the only really good building on the block would be possible from a marketing and leasing point of view. So he spent the money. And it worked. The place is full.

Ada Louise Huxtable made a comment in 1976 about your work in the Pennzoil Building and its economic one-upmanship. She said that the tallest building in a city may have a temporary advantage, but a notable building has a permanent one. Why do you think that some architects decry this way of thinking as commercial, as sort of dirty?

Because it is a whore's business, designing to please the client. The client, being a developer, has only one interest, and that's rent. And with that interest at heart, the hard thing to learn – and Gerry was the first to learn it – is that when you build a better building, you'll get better rent. What really launched our career as designers of office towers was Paul Goldberger's article in the *New York Times*, "The New American Skyscraper." Oh, the article was famous. But the obvious point – that if you pay more for design, you'll get more money in the long run – has been Gerry's principle ever since.

But a lot of other developers never got that message, even during the 1980s boom. They may have put a little glitz into the buildings, but only because they were told they had to.

That's right. However, there were people who copied Gerry, like Prentiss Properties, the developer in Dallas who worked with us on the Crescent and Momentum Place. And George Klein here in New York who brought me in to do Times Square for Park Tower Realty.

Hines was, in a way, the best kind of patron, because he found other patrons like Hugh Liedtke and Jack Bowen. When he saw a patron-type client, he knew they would work well with me. I mean, he's that smart. He only gave me one cheap building, in Denver. It was a success, all right, but I was never pleased with it.

We asked Louis Sklar of the Hines office how they chose architects. He said that some clients are the right ones to put together with a Philip Johnson, others are not.

Oh, there's no question that he wouldn't pick me for a job for which I am unsuited. But why he's never used me in Germany, for instance, is odd. I think it's like working for a university. You work for a certain amount, and then something happens. It's as if someone says, "We don't want to be known as the Johnson firm."

You wanted round columns in the lobby of Transco but ended up with hexagonal ones. Was it too expensive to make them round?

Yes, well when Louis Sklar wasn't looking, we got round ones in the Lipstick building. Gerry made that decision. Now it's much harder, because there isn't much money in real estate development these days, so Gerry isn't interested anymore.

Well, the market's very quiet.

Yes. Euphemism number sixty-two-and-a-half. Well, he's working in Europe. It's the only place any developer is working. But he has that extra taste that enables him to make these decisions. The Lipstick building is full. When we first built the RepublicBank, I asked Gerry if the building was full, because it was right around the crash of the real estate market. He told me, "It's full, Philip, but I won't tell you how." He didn't get the rents he would have expected, I suppose.

So Liedtke's a good client. Bowen was a good client. The architect is the last one to know what the real relationship is. People

What really launched our career as designers of office towers was Goldberger's article in the *New York Times*, "The New American Skyscraper."

who may look good to me as patrons afterwards are really the result of Hines's smart policy.

Pennzoil Place is directly across the street from your more recent RepublicBank. Is that a coincidence?

That is a very interesting story. Originally I thought I'd build a building similar to Pennzoil, because they were to be placed together. I thought they'd make a great symphony. Gerry just exploded. "The whole point is to sell this as a new building, you fool. It has to contrast."

Republic was one of the worst clients Gerry ever had, he told me. They just fought all the time. Republic's headquarters were in Dallas. And Dallas and Houston are rather like St. Paul and Minneapolis – that is, they don't speak to each other. So a Repub-

How Gerry got away with that little piece of expensiveness, I'll never know. That building couldn't have been cheap. Look at it! It's the best building.

lic executive had come down to Houston from that "other city" and was telling Gerry what to do. How Gerry got away with that little piece of expensiveness I'll never know. That building couldn't have been cheap. Look at it! It's the best building – it's my favorite building – in Houston.

More so than Transco?

In a way, yes. The reason I like RepublicBank better than Transco is I feel it's more original. There was more thought behind it. It makes a unique picture. After all, the tower of Transco, although it's very thin and very graceful, is really derivative of a stone building, the Nebraska State Capitol in Lincoln by Goodhue. It is not an imitation, but derivative.

I picked up the theme, of course, from Henry-Russell Hitchcock's book on Dutch gables. I read too much of it, maybe, but anyhow, it rubbed off, and I enjoyed using that theme. However, nobody ever used a gable like that. And especially they never tiered a gable. That made absolutely no sense in historical terms, you see. So the only "historical" gables were the little pinnacles on each bay. For selling real estate, the stepping does not seem very logical, because the rooms get smaller as they go higher. The whole trick of a developer is to get more volume on the top because that's where the views are. People always want to be on the top. But Gerry was very generous and very supportive of this odd shape, so he let us go ahead with it.

But there's a very strange thing about that gable. In the Dutch and Flemish gables of the seventeenth century, for example, you look right at the gable. But in the RepublicBank, the gable runs the long way to your first view, so it's only the steps that you see, those odd steps that we added to give Hugh Liedtke his view from Pennzoil Place.

So that was a combination of starting with a thing that was already in my mind from a book, plus the idea of stepping it for one man's view. It is so odd that it led to an original and yet very interesting solution. More and more, it was Hitchcock's favorite building of mine, and I think I see why. There's no question that that's going to be the most remembered of the buildings in Houston after people absorb the obvious prettiness of Transco, the fact that it stands all out by itself, which is very rare.

But the RepublicBank also has all kinds of references to different eras. There's a little Louis Sullivan, from the early banks. There's the "Bridge of Sighs" from Richardson's Allegheny County Courthouse going between the two buildings. Is this the fever pitch of your historicism?

I wonder. I think so. It's the most successful. It's funny, the best thing about it, if you want to pick out specific features, is the fact that it's stepped. Liedtke's office in Pennzoil faces the stepped top. He can look right past the RepublicBank building because the top steps back right there. He still has his great view.

We showed the plan to Mr. Liedtke before we went into construction. We asked him, "Can you see how we've changed this building just so that your office will get a good view?"

Your work in the late 1970s and early 1980s, when you were working for Gerry Hines, shows a wide range. RepublicBank, compared with 101 California in San Francisco, is more historically styled.

REPUBLICBANK DETAIL OF GABLED ROOF

It's a matter of the client, you see. Gerry Hines was in a bind. When building 101 California, he had to meet the particular demands of a tenant who really controlled the financing of that project. And so he brought me in. There was another architect doing a different scheme that the client could choose, which is a

PPG practically refused to build it. So I suggested we mock up a big enough piece, and then we go across the river. And that persuaded them.

very rare arrangement. The client picked me. It was quite a difficult building to design, primarily because of cost.

In the RepublicBank, I felt I knew how to make a difference in Houston, because I had done it in other buildings. That's actually my third design for that site. I did a modern version – it went diagonally through the entire block. The longest diagonal was 400 feet, a really amazing building. It didn't fly for some reason. Gerry was very disappointed. But he also liked the final version. I really had no patron on the RepublicBank except Gerry. And he was completely supportive.

The PPG Building is very different stylistically from your other postmodern work. Is that difference because of the glass surface?

The client was very interested in showing off glass since that was part of their business. We made full-scale mock-ups of the bottom of the building and looked at it from across the river from up at their plants. That's when we got the theory of the white and black. Dark glass buildings are universal – but so awful and threatening. I asked, "Would white work?" And they were horrified. They said, "You don't put a white cage over a black building!" They practically refused to build it. So I suggested we mock up a big enough piece, and then we both go across the river to look at it. And that persuaded them.

That's similar to the Crystal Cathedral, which is a white cage with glass, at least on the interior.

That's right. But that's white for another reason, for reflection.

How did you decide on the Gothic forms for PPG?

The tower idea came from the Cathedral of Learning, the famous Gothic tower at the University of Pittsburgh. The idea of the series of towers came from Richardson's Allegheny County

PITTSBURGH SKYLINE SHOWING PPG TOWER

PPG DETAIL OF FACADE

THE WINTERGARDEN

Courthouse. I knew you would see PPG coming through the tunnel most people use to enter downtown Pittsburgh. I was still into the Transco thing, where glass could be stone. And glass could be used with the Gothic. Here I could use a square tower and make it high enough. That was one trouble with Pennzoil Place; it's just not high enough.

How did you come to the decision to create satellite buildings around PPG's central tower, instead of incorporating all the space into a single building?

Oh, it's a village idea. A cathedral and the low buildings around its base make a square. Well, the truth was that they had

You can copy the Parthenon, just as they did in Nashville. But it's – I'm sorry, it ain't there. A copy just doesn't do it.

five acres. What the heck was I going to do with five acres? I suggested that we build a plaza and the lower buildings, which could be rented out.

Had PPG originally wanted to keep all the property just for itself?

Oh, no, never. They were planning on renting all of the space except for the tower. At first it was difficult. It's all right now; it filled up. Now, of course, the president of PPG says it's the only building he wanted – he couldn't imagine how it could be so good. But at the time, they were very dubious.

Is the obelisk at the center of the plaza your design?

Yes, it's my design – a Napoleonic obelisk. Since I couldn't get anybody to do anything that I would trust, I decided to build an obelisk. It's simply an early nineteenth-century shape.

Did the client have much input?

Didn't even know what was going on.

But why did they come to me in the first place? Because really, they never liked me. The president of the company got so mad one day he took a plane all the way up here to tell me. Gerry has always liked high ceilings; I used ten-foot ceilings in AT&T. So I told the PPG people, this is a headquarters building. You ought to have ten-foot ceilings. Well, their cost people got to them and told them they were out of their minds. Apparently that change in ceiling height jumps up the cost of the building by ten percent,

just like that. I had told them it wouldn't cost that much more, but what did I know?

The year 1979 seemed to be a high point in your career: in addition to PPG, you were doing the AT&T Building, 101 California, and the Transco Tower.

The same time. Can you imagine? Fantastic. Well, you get these spates of activity.

But among all those projects, you like RepublicBank the most?

I don't think I have that kind of favorite. I've liked it much better than I thought I would, even though I don't like postmodern anymore. I don't like the AT&T Building now.

I like the idea of PPG, because there's no detail. Detailing is where you get into trouble. Why is PPG Gothic? It's just this pointed thing. It's just decoration. And somehow I can defend that as better. In the AT&T Building, I used Romanesque-cushioned capitals. Well, they weren't very good, because there's something in the air of proportion of detail that simply will not translate. You can copy the Parthenon, just as they did in Nashville. But it's – I'm sorry, it ain't there. A copy just doesn't do it.

What does it is something else. I always use the analogy of Stravinsky. He took anything from anywhere. But it's still modern music. He was a very good modern musician, I would say. His use of older elements was unimportant. What was important was the total result.

Would you say that your tall office buildings are all somewhat related to the Eliel Saarinen design for the Tribune Tower competition in Chicago?

The Saarinen tower certainly started it all. But the best man, by far, was Goodhue. His entry in the Tribune Tower competition I consider superior to Saarinen's. I never knew him personally. But the Nebraska capitol is more what I was thinking of when I was doing my designs.

Did you begin to have doubts about postmodernism when you were building Transco?

No, that came later, after the great success of AT&T. Then I got absolutely fascinated by Eisenman and Frank Gehry. The work of Frank Stella is influencing me now.

Given the constraints of the real estate business, can something like deconstructivism work in commercial development?

Deconstructivism is a limiting word. We pick these bad words because we need a label. Anyway, today there are no developers to convince. I'm not sure we could. But they can still build a box if they want to. Who is going to stop them?

ELEVATOR LOBBY AT 500 BOYLSTON STREET, BOSTON

Urbane Landscape

Forth Worth Water Garden
Fort Worth, Texas
1970-1975

University of St. Thomas
Houston, Texas
1957

Roofless Church
New Harmony, Indiana
1960

Nuclear Reactor
Rehovot, Israel
1960

Philip Johnson freely admits his love of landscape, even as he allows that some people praise his work in this area at the critical expense of his work in architecture. Johnson sees architecture as broadly defined. His work clearly blurs the line between the "two" arts of architecture and landscape.

His work in landscape is diverse, ranging from the intimate garden at The Museum of Modern Art to his sprawling estate in New Canaan. Some of his best urban landscapes are in Texas, namely, the Fort Worth Water Garden (1970-75) and Thanksgiving Square in Dallas (1971-77). These are both playful but refined public spaces, an oxymoronic combination coming from anyone else but somehow almost obvious from a man who lives in one of the most urbane country houses ever conceived.

You've said that the Fort Worth Water Garden is one of your favorite projects. How did you get the commission?

Through Ruth Carter Stevenson, who was the head of the Amon Carter Foundation. Her father's favorite child. She asked me, "What would you do, Philip, if you could turn five blocks run down by slums into a city park?" I did a design for a park that she didn't particularly like, and then we developed this one, which she was crazy about.

The first one was a great fort with turrets at the corners that you could go into and from which you could look down at the water. It was a protected area. It had more presence in the city, I felt.

Was she more worried about the safety implications?

Well, no. It was just the look. It didn't seem like Fort Worth to her. She pictured the wide-open West and all that. We ended up with a plan where you so casually come in from all sides.

The garden is a wonderful mix of environments. It feels as though you have stumbled upon a piece of the Adirondacks set in a very urban backdrop.

It wasn't the Adirondacks I had in mind. I was trying to work out a new civic experience, based on fake nature that would be amusing to people, in as many different forms as possible. One of the forms was water, which I used in three opposing ways. The first was a perfectly plain pattern. The second was the great cavern where water crashes down on you, and that's the most exciting, because of the noise and the "dangerous" feel of going down the unprotected steps into a chasm. The third was a spray garden – just a normal garden where it's cooler. Fort Worth is a hot town. It's a little cooler where that spray is than anywhere else. So with the three conditions of water, and with the fake mountain, built of steps of concrete, I felt that you had that wonderful sense of being in the Adirondacks, but small. So all those things were partially a

reduction of a large landscape, but also the creation of a city square. There is a pedestrian gathering-place right in the middle of the park. I wanted it for action. I wanted it for plays and speeches and public protests. The speaker can back up against the mountain and speak to the assembled multitude.

You see the trees, you see the obvious mountain, and the minute you get in, you discover, all right, that rushing water cavern, or pit, or whatever it is. So you see the variety. I suppose Dis-

The great cemeteries of the late nineteenth century, with their feeling of mourning all around, are very sentimental. A leftover, of course, from the sublime.

ney inspired me a little bit, but I wanted to get the feeling of experiment and discovery. The little paths go around behind the mountain. You can, of course, climb straight up the face. But then due to the relation of the step to its height, it would be a little too dangerous to climb without the path. It's hard, because the steps are so high, 20 inches. But you can go up a side way, a little path. Then you can come down into the smooth-water area 20 feet below. To arrive there you go down through a little, tiny way and then all of a sudden, apart from everything, is this great place of water surrounded by trees. All these different experiences – it gives you something to do, it gives you an experience.

Did you anticipate that?

Yes, but not at that time. The trees were just fuzzy little things on my map, you know, and there was water in all its aspects: quiet water and really vigorous water.

The sharp angles and the steep steps of landscape were the features that seemed most Philip Johnson to us.

The angles are, believe it or not, absolutely random. I had kids in the office doing them. I just did the orchestrating, and the kids worked hardest on this effect with the engineer.

They look like steps, but in fact they're not.

No, because there is no place to go up there.

Were you influenced by historic models in this design?

I got the idea of all these secret little walkways from the Buttes-Chaumont in Paris. It isn't as well known as it should be,

but it's one of the great parks of all time. It was built in the 1860s under Napoleon. It has fake caverns, and little bridges, a little fake mountain, and a little lookout on the top, and the little hanging bridge that you can go across to another mountain. Even Disneyland isn't quite fun enough, when you think of the Buttes-Chaumont. I mean, you don't have a big mountain, or the big tunnel going through a big fake hill. It gives the same feeling as another great garden in Paris, Père Lachaise Cemetery. Mount Auburn Cemetery in Cambridge is another wonderful walk, by the way. The great cemeteries of the late nineteenth century, with their feeling of mourning all around, are very sentimental. A leftover, of course, from the sublime.

I recently heard the sublime defined as pretty horrible things that are seen from a very safe place. That definition works here. The great "horror" of my chasm is tempered because you're perfectly safe walking down those steps. But you don't feel that way, because there's all the water rushing around you, and there are no handrails or anything. It's just marvelous. That garden is really, perhaps, one of my great successes. But it has nothing to do with the other gardens I've done, at MoMA or in Dallas. Thanksgiving Square in Dallas is an open, public square where you just walk in. It's just a garden in the middle of the city.

Had you originally intended to put more water in the Fort Worth garden?

No, no, just the three pools.

Were there any particular difficulties working with this site?

The highway behind the garden is going. It will go underground. Already been approved by the state.

Fort Worth is a very hot climate. Did that affect your design?

Sure, because the water is cool. You can go down there. You get splashed down, and that cools you off at once. And then the rush of the water makes its own wind.

So you were thinking in processional terms?

Oh, heavens, yes. From the street, the whole thing focuses on the central square.

We were struck by how different in feeling it is from your garden at The Museum of Modern Art.

It's the opposite; the problem was different. The Museum of Modern Art kept the public very much out in the middle of a busy city. In Fort Worth we wanted people to filter in.

The Water Garden has elements of the "safe danger" you have talked about in the Glass House. For example, the steps seem so

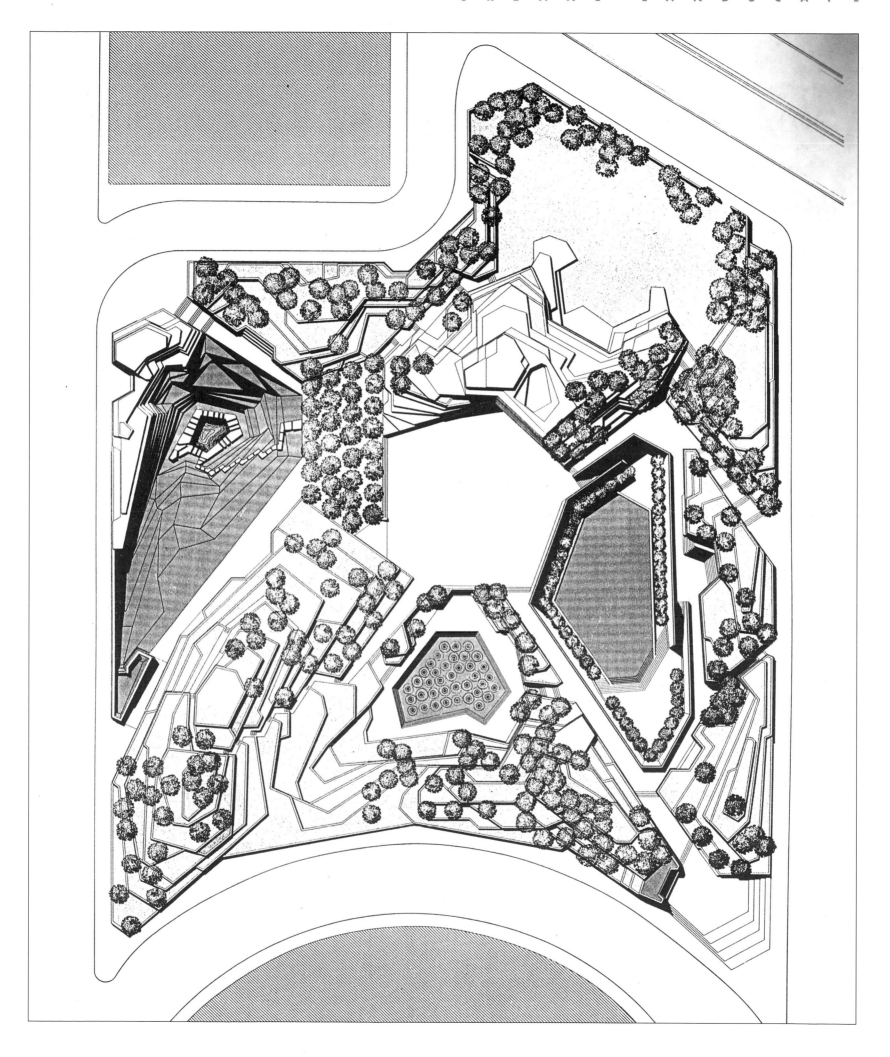

FORT WORTH WATER GARDEN, PLAN

steep. Was that something you did consciously – make them look like you can climb them, even though you can't?

You can climb them if you're young. The old can watch. The size of the steps are 20 inches by 16 inches. In other words, you sit always on a 20-inch seat, which is perfect for perching, not lying or sitting, but for perching. If you want to climb, 20 inches, you can do it easily, if you're young. I really only want kids climbing those things. Also, you get this 20-inch feeling all around, like topographical layers on a map, and that gives you a very recognizable layering.

Have you ever been to temples in Mexico? They're very scary to climb straight up. So is this. But it doesn't hurt anything. It's like my Lincoln Kirstein Tower at the Glass House. It's almost scary to climb up. Everybody turns around at the halfway point, except kids. But I wasn't thinking about my principles of near or safe danger at this time. Some little bit of titillation is necessary, you see. People wouldn't go down into the whirlpool if it did not

> ## You think Le Nôtre wasn't an architect? And Capability Brown? I mean, that's all architecture. I don't find the line drawn anywhere.

feel a little dangerous. Well, maybe not dangerous, but adventurous. Even in Disneyland, they use a lot of words like "adventure."

But how do you create adventure? How do you titillate without scaring people?

Scary is all right. You certainly get scared on roller coasters. You have to feel adventurous, but really you're in no danger at all. Same thing, climbing here. That's an adventure, see? Kids climb the "mountain." That's the only way you can get to the high point to see the garden. It's all an exploration. And that's why I made some areas dark, because it's more secret. You go through the dark, and then you come out into the placid pool. There is a peak and there is a pit – the high and then the low. And the access is really very easy. Things would be too hard to get to, if I had made it any more circuitous.

Was this a fun project for you?

Of course. As some people say, I'm a better landscape architect than I am an architect.

Well, people say that. Do you say that?

Hope not. To me, it's one art. You think Le Nôtre wasn't an architect? And Capability Brown? I mean, that's all architecture. I don't find the line drawn anywhere. But I have been very successful with these two, the Fort Worth garden and The Museum of Modern Art garden.

Tell us a little about your other city garden, Thanksgiving Square in Dallas?

I'm working with the owners of that now. It's owned by the city. But it's run by the man who founded it – Peter Stewart. We're putting a new end on it. As with the Fort Worth Water Garden, I did it as a flight from the city. Except no adventure here; it's a refuge. That's where Ada Louise Huxtable got me in the *New York Times*. She said Thanksgiving Square goes slightly above the street, four feet plus, so it's anti-public. And I said, "What does Central Park do? Exactly the same. You get in at the corner, same thing that you do here."

By "anti-public" does she mean exclusionary?

Yes, she means exclusionary. I should have people just wandering through it like Bryant Park in New York City. Connect with the streets.

Both the Fort Worth Water Garden and Thanksgiving Square use a lot of the same means, like the water and the feeling of a descent into a private garden. In Thanksgiving Square there's just a walk; no steps at all. Today steps are, of course, frowned upon: they are not acceptable; they are not politically correct. Isn't it infuriating? Because steps, of course, are the essence of *architecture*! Well, the Water Garden wouldn't be acceptable today to the city. It is all steps.

You'd have to put a ramp going all the way down to the water.

Well, then you'd have to protect the ramps by railings and everything – the whole thing.

Do you have a favorite garden, apart from the ones that you've created yourself?

Of course! Le Nôtre at Vaux-le-Vicomte. And of course, the English gardens. My favorite, in fact, is an English garden in Germany, Wörlitz, a mile or so outside Dessau. It is from around 1800 – that great period. It is an enormous property, with lots of water. You can pull yourself across on that little barge, from island to island, and then you're walking along, and all of a sudden you come to a mountain! All artificial. The edge of the garden is marked only by a range of mountains, maybe all of 20-feet high. So it's an enclosed garden.

That's *the* leading German garden. Think how little that influenced the Bauhaus – it drives you crazy! It's the opposite end of the spectrum.

AERIAL VIEW OF WATER GARDEN

Since the garden was in Dessau, certainly everyone at the Bauhaus would have been familiar with it, wouldn't they?

No, no. They didn't have the faintest idea where it was! And it's not more than ten minutes away from the Bauhaus. I found out about the garden from a historian in Berlin who specialized in the eighteenth century.

Was it considered to be too tacky, because it was artificial?

Well, artificial, yes, but it wasn't anti-bourgeois.

But people at the Bauhaus rejected Wörlitz?

They were uninterested in a romantic, sentimental garden.

145

In 1957 Johnson was commissioned to design a master plan for the University of St. Thomas in Houston. What resulted was an ode to Mies van der Rohe, but not without a clear Johnsonian edge. While starkly modern in style, the overall plan of the buildings and connecting arcade (which Johnson refers to as one building) is, according to the architect, an idea out of Thomas Jefferson's plan for the University of Virginia in Charlottesville. The campus is, like Jefferson's, as much a landscape as it is a built work. While Johnson did not design all the buildings behind the arcade, he now has the commission, more than 35 years later, to design a chapel to be the "centerpiece" for the composition.

This conversation also includes two projects that may be somewhat less well known: the Nuclear Reactor in Rehovot, Israel, and the Roofless Church in New Harmony, Indiana, both completed in 1960. These two projects, though wildly different in program, share formal qualities. They are exquisite outdoor rooms as well as objects in the landscape.

We've heard that the president of the University of St. Thomas, Dr. Joseph McFadden, wanted to give you an honorary degree to get you to come back to design more for the campus.

Yes. He came up here with his brilliant fund-raiser. They had realized that you can't have a Catholic school without a chapel – a contradiction in terms.

Your original design for the campus had a chapel, but you didn't get a chance to build it. Did the school run out of money?

Yes. Of course, Catholics now are not church-minded. They're more political. Yes, political correctness has reached the Catholic Church, even if certain other things haven't. The university has now raised money for two buildings: the science building and the chapel.

Which buildings did you build in the original 1957 plan?

I did the master plan, the little auditorium, and some of the other buildings, but not the library at the end of the arcade.

The story from Dr. McFadden was that you insisted on building the entire arcade, even with no buildings, out as far as possible so that future presidents could not mess up the plan.

And they didn't.

How did you get the original commission?

Oh, that was pure Mrs. John de Menil. She had a great friend, Mary Callery, who had the greatest collection of Picassos. The

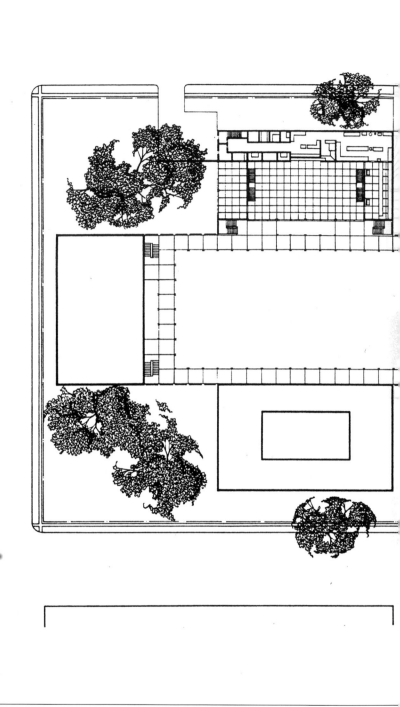

UNIVERSITY OF ST. THOMAS, CAMPUS PLAN

Menils were visiting Mrs. Callery in New York, and they mentioned that they needed an architect. Mrs. Callery said, "Well, a great friend of mine is Philip Johnson. And he's young, and he'll go down there and give you what you want." And I built their house in Houston. Then the Menils were patrons of the University of St. Thomas.

How did you know Mrs. Callery?

I knew Mrs. Callery through Alfred Barr at The Museum of Modern Art. She was a sculptor and she had a great collection. That's what Alfred was after.

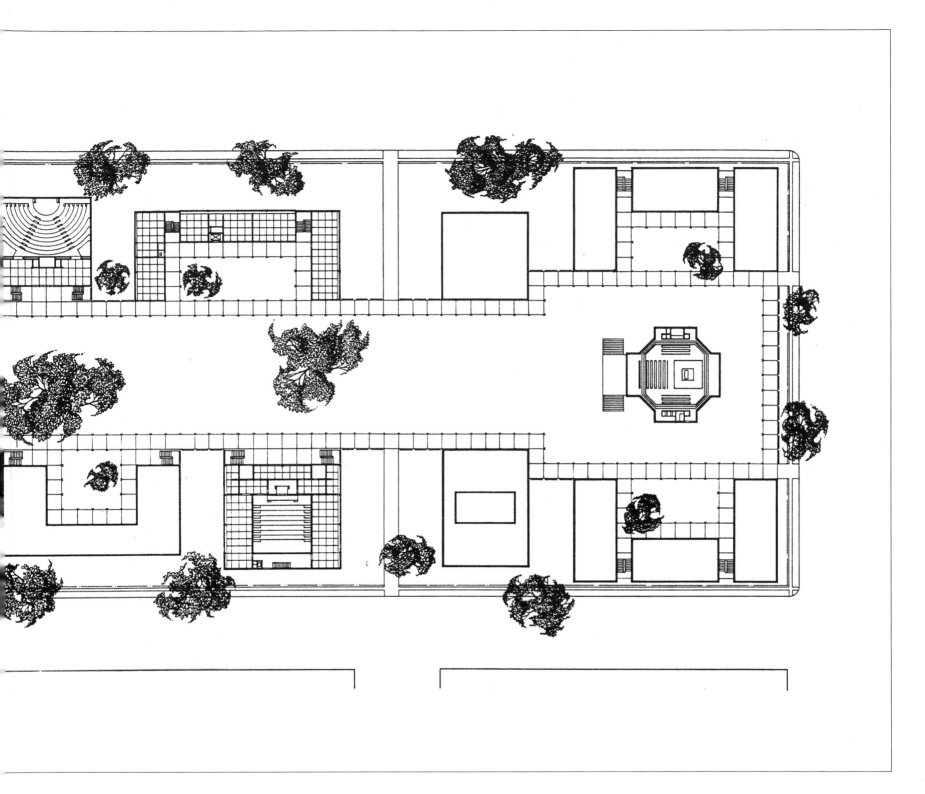

Anyway, Mrs. de Menil was running the art history department of the University of St. Thomas. She's a runner of things, and very, very good. Her museum, the Menil Collection, is maybe the finest private museum in the country. It's a lovely place.

How did you get dragged back to Houston to do the church? Supposedly, you were no longer traveling for work.

Dr. McFadden said, "We'll get the money." Now where have I heard that before? And "Don't you want to finish the campus?" I mean, simple as that. And I said, "Well, A, we dreamed of finishing it. But B, the only kind of building that I'd like to build, since

I'm not working very hard now, is a church." And he said, "Here's your chance." So I did.

Has there been opposition to your design for the chapel? It is hardly traditional, not to mention that it's quite different from your original campus.

No, the school thought it was absolutely fantastic. Well, of course, at that time they didn't have enough money to build it, so it was easy to say that. And McFadden is such a nice man. Still, it is meant to be different and show its date. But it's very polite to the rest of the campus.

McFadden takes a little bit of credit for getting you back into full-time practice.

That's right. He and his commission contributed a good deal to my recovery.

There's another little thing. It's called P-r-o-z-a-c.

Certainly, the style of that chapel is drastically different from the surrounding campus.

Oh, yes. But you can do that with a church. It doesn't have to be the same architecture as the rest of the campus, any more than Jefferson's rotunda at the University of Virginia has to be like the little study houses that flank it.

But do you agree with the idea of maintaining the basic form of the campus as a modern campus?

Oh, absolutely. The whole campus is really only one building. And this chapel is the part of that building that is the point of difference – a little heart to the colonnade like the portico in the Rotunda in Charlottesville.

It actually is similar to the way you laid out the Roofless Church in Indiana.

It is! That's right. An altar at the end and a processional. The nuclear reactor I did is the same thing; it has a court. There is a similarity to all of them. I think I got it, clearly, from Jefferson. If I'd had the library to build at St. Thomas, I would have made that building monumental.

Meaning you would have made it much larger than the one there now and have it stand out?

Oh, yes. So it would be the other anchor, yes. In fact, it ended up exactly the same as the composition at the University of Virginia. They got McKim, Mead & White to do the ending there. But of course, what Jefferson meant to do was to have his campus face out into America. You look out over all Virginia. Closing that in was not a good idea.

When are you planning on proceeding into construction with the new building?

It is delayed due to money. The building will cost less than $2 million to build. However, you've got to endow the building, you have to pay for the land and maintenance. I asked them, "Why don't you build it, then? You've got $3 million already." But they have to wait. Of course, Harvard waits for endowments to be funded, as well.

Do you have a favorite religious building that you've designed?

Well, there's always the next one – well, yes, I'd say the St. Thomas chapel.

We thought the Crystal Cathedral might be your favorite, but then it's a very different program – a large church, not a chapel.

Right, it's very different. This is a little chapel that fits in a little area that needs decorating, God knows. The campus very badly needs a focal point. Of course, they won't do me the favor of taking down the trees that block the view. I mean, trees are fine. But to bury the thing in a forest! For heaven's sake, you don't build a campus and then put trees in the way – you have got all the shade in the world. If you get sunny on one side, go over to the other side.

Dr. McFadden had mentioned that there is a large fourteenth-century crucifix that Mrs. de Menil has donated for the interior. Does that in any way contradict the style of the chapel?

Oh, no, because I planned it for placement over the altar.

The Roofless Church in New Harmony, Indiana and the nuclear reactor in Israel are curiously similar.

Yes, they're exactly the same. They were conceived at about the same time. They're both symmetrical, they both have an entrance at the short end, the cult object at the other, and of course, the court.

Were you thinking in terms of a Greek temple?

No, it's more like a Roman atrium, much more Roman than Greek. I don't know any Greek enclosed places.

It seemed to be similar to walking into the Parthenon, with Pallas Athena right there.

Oh, Lord, no. The procession was entirely different. I mean, look at Choisy. There you come in from the *back* of the Parthenon, and then you go around the Parthenon, past the Erechtheum and the Athena Parthenos, the big statue. The Parthenon is just a ghost up at your right. And then you turn the corner and face down. It is just the opposite. Those Greek processions had nothing to do with the Roman, which were just much more head-on. And then, of course, during Renaissance times, symmetry became an absolute.

You are not known for building much outside of the United States.

Well, I did the museum in Bielefeld, Germany in the 1960s. And of course there were houses overseas, like the Boissonnas House in Cap Bénat, France. Today I am building in Berlin. When I built the nuclear reactor in Israel, I was very fortunate.

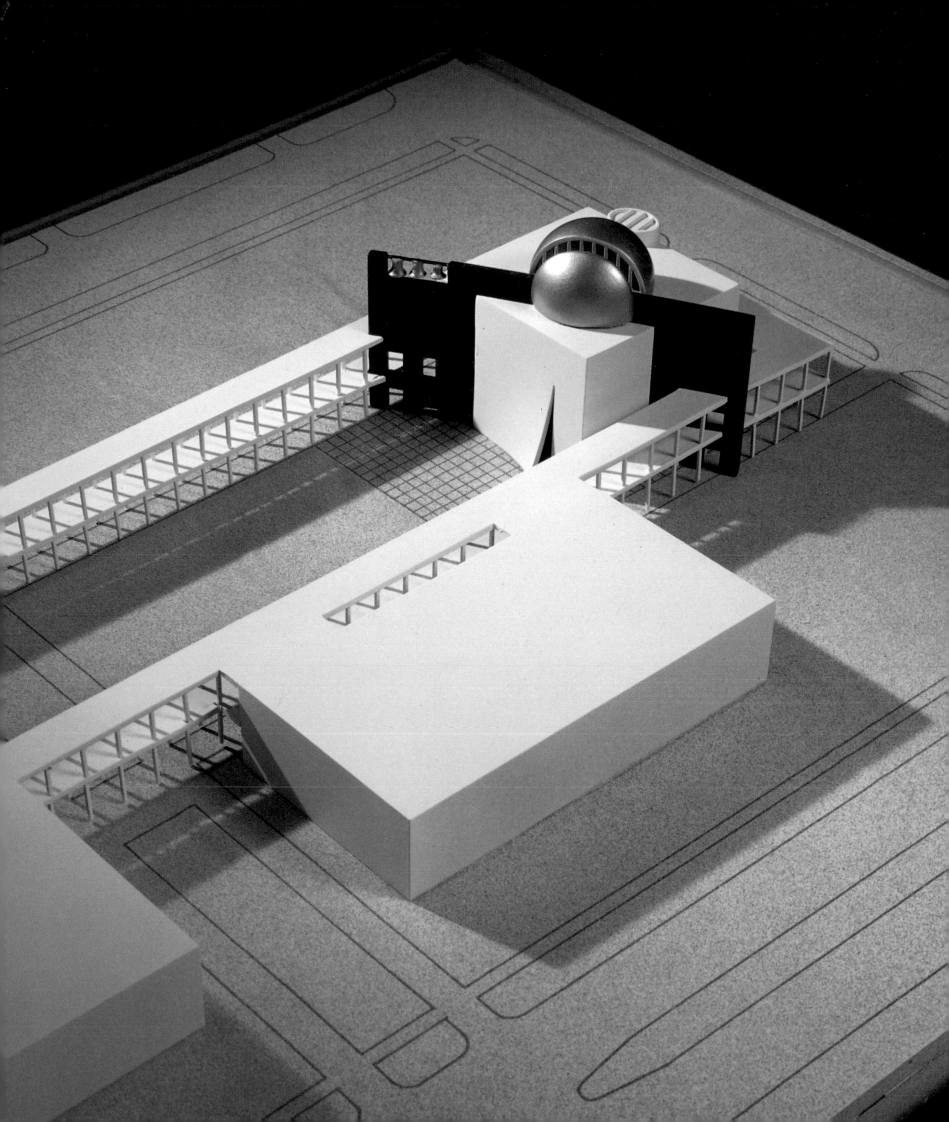

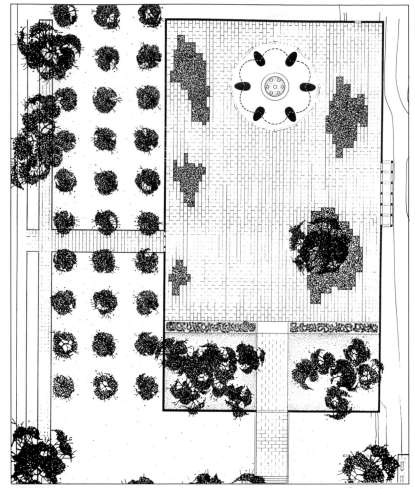

ROOFLESS CHURCH, PLAN

I hadn't the slightest idea what I was building. What does a nuclear reactor look like? I didn't do the inside – naturally, I don't know what all that stuff is. But I worked with the client. They wanted so many laboratories.

So it's a research institute?

Yes. It's an experimental facility. It is not a working reactor. It's a university teaching and research building.

It's much more decorative than anything at MIT.

That's right. It's a very pretty building, out in the desert. Of course, the land around it is now covered with ticky-tacky houses! There was just one olive tree on the site originally. Just a tree in the desert. The shadow on the building and the isolation of the site were major aspects of the design.

How in the world did you get a commission for a nuclear reactor, in Israel no less? Did you know someone there? Or did you just get a call out of the blue?

There's a genius in Israel named Shimon Peres. He's now the foreign minister, and he is just great. He wanted this to be something worthy. They later put a picture of it on their pound note. But how Shimon Peres had heard of me, I have no idea.

Well, your name had been in the papers.

Not in those days.

In the 1950s? Mrs. de Menil knew to use you.

But she met me through Mary Callery. Well, the first thing I knew, a guy came in here and said, "I'm from Israel, and we're looking for a man to do a nuclear reactor, but it isn't just that. It's really a civic monument, a national monument. There is no good architecture in Israel, and there should be. Maybe you, Mr. Johnson, could do this?" All I knew, a guy came in. I can hardly believe it now. And he – his name was Gideon Ziv – became my local architect. I never saw him after that. He never surfaced again. But who did surface was Shimon himself.

So it was really his commission.

It was his commission. He was the head of the army in those days. And armies do funny things in new countries.

Did the client have any input in terms of the design?

Not a bit. They didn't even present it. They just approved it. Then they went on to build it, the way you should do buildings.

Did Shimon Peres come to New York to find you?

No. I worked for a long time before I met Shimon, until I went over to Israel on my first visit. But I never saw the site. I've never seen the building, even though I've been back to Israel a lot.

You never went to see the building?

No, I don't know what got into me.

After I had designed the nuclear reactor I got to know Shimon Peres quite well. He actually came out to the Glass House once just to see it. We sat down to talk, and he said, "When am I going to see you in Israel again?" And I told him I had made no plans to visit there. He said, "Well, come back and build something in Israel!" And I said, "I'd love to, Mr. Minister, but, ah, what should I build?" He said, "What do you *want* to build? I've got the marble, I have the workmen, the armies. I have everything all set. Just say what you want. We need *everything* in Israel! So please come to Israel and build!" That's what I call a pitch!

Later on I designed the airport at Lod near Tel Aviv, which they didn't get money enough to build. That was a direct commission from Shimon.

So you maintained a relationship with him.

Oh, he's a wonderful man. The kind of man you just wish were running the world, you know. Lovely.

NUCLEAR REACTOR AT REHOVOT, ISRAEL. PHOTOGRAPH BY ARNOLD NEWMAN

The Consistent Chameleon

Architecture, like art and literature, is a constant revolution. Some periods seem to last forever, and others are discarded almost as quickly as yesterday's newspaper. The International Style, Johnson points out, has lasted longer than the Renaissance. Art deco was a quick and beautiful flash in the pan. But change is a constant.

Johnson says that in the 1930s he was a "true believer" in the International Style. If you asked him in the 1970s, he'd tell you it was a bore. Today he's concentrating feverishly on a style that of yet has no fixed title, a style in the state of flux – postmodernism now only a mile marker 20 miles past. He seems to revel in this pace and in his ability to shift from one ideology to the next – his entire life's work becoming one long experiment.

In this chapter, when Johnson says he's "not a big time original architect" and that most criticisms of him are correct, we see a glimpse of his humbler side. On the other hand, he swiftly discounts a connection to a pop sensibility and strongly defends his more humorous work as closer to a Duchampian irony. Which persona are we to believe?

You have made several major shifts in design direction over your career. In your experience, what are the first signs that a cultural or architectonic shift is about to occur? For example, you had mentioned being "bored with the box" as your main reason for moving away from modernism.

Well, these terms are all invented afterwards, of course. It's all Monday morning quarterbacking. It happens in your stomach long before. And later you've got to put a word on it or a reason for it. The worst part is the label. "Deconstructivism," the "International Style" – it hasn't any meaning whatsoever. But without a name it won't go into the press, and the press sets what happens. It doesn't have to be the popular press – it could be the journals – but it's still that.

But how do you know things are really changing? Do you just have a feeling in your gut?

Like everything else, you feel dissatisfied and want to go in another direction. Why, I don't know. Most people don't feel it. When you say it happens, I wonder how external it is and how much is just the labeling. Did deconstruction really happen or is it something we just pulled out of whole cloth?

Well, frequently you also get a term that encompasses a lot of different stuff.

That's right.

Let's start at the beginning with your interest in modernism. It seems that much of the International Style focused on creating

buildings, both offices and housing, cheaply. Did you feel that by building your New Canaan house, with its great expense and detail, that you were somehow violating the original intent or purpose of that style?

Of course. But I always did. I did it in the 1920s when I was in Berlin where there were two camps. There was one gathered around Mies van der Rohe and one gathered around Gropius. As modern architects, they both were represented in all exhibitions, like the *Weissenhofsiedlung* in Stuttgart. Or in Mies's show of 1931. That was *the* great show of modern architecture in Berlin. Of course, Gropius and Breuer were there. But we had that fundamental difference. We, Mies and I, believed in the art of architecture, and they believed in the sociological importance of architecture. And since Gropius was not a great designer, he naturally stressed the sociological side. This dichotomy is still present.

On the left, they believe housing for the poor is the only thing to build. On the right, they say the modern style is cheaper to build. So you still have these opposing things. The Communist Party has disappeared, and they were the people behind the sociological approach. They called us *all* bourgeois.

That's right, you were sellouts. You still have elements of that in architectural schools.

Oh schools, they're politically correct.

It does seem like the architecture gets lost in the process.

Of course it does.

When you wrote The International Style *in the 1930s, did you already see the debate of modernism between those two poles?*

Sure. Our book was written as a piece of propaganda against

I wonder how external it is and how much is just the labeling. Did deconstruction really happen or is it something we just pulled out of whole cloth?

the sociological. "We have an architecture still" is the last sentence in the book.

In The International Style, *there's an interesting comment in Alfred Barr's own preface. He talks about how the architecture is Gothic in terms of ideology but really Greek in terms of stylistics.*

190 SOUTH LASALLE STREET, CHICAGO

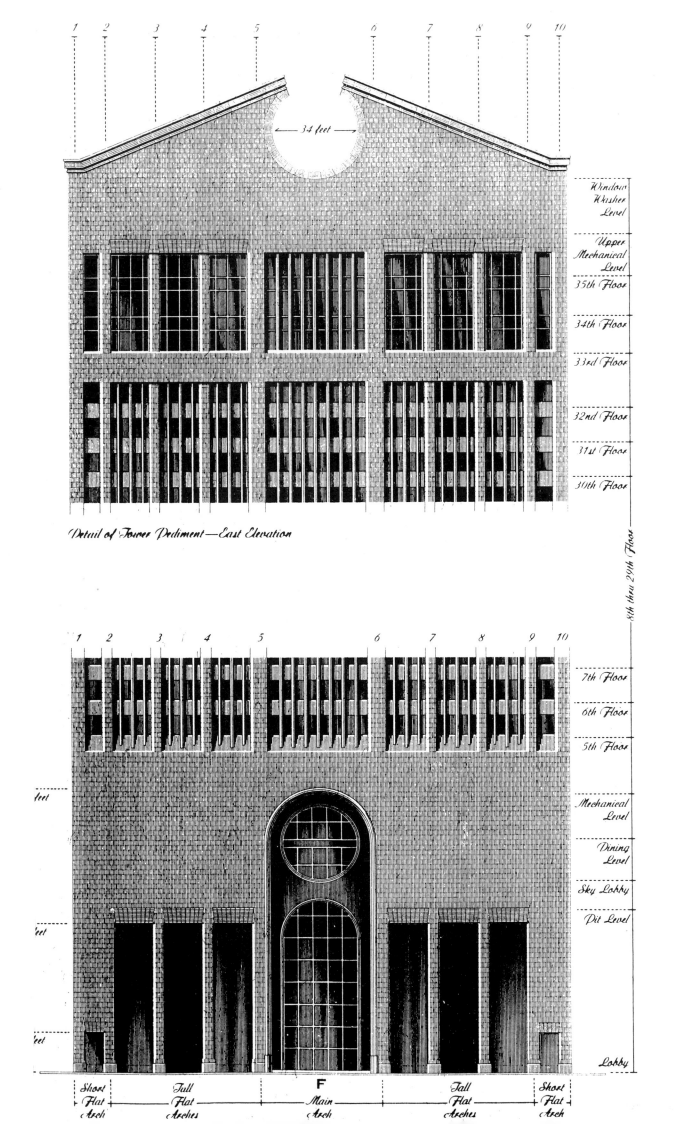

1   2   3   4   5   6   7   8   9   10

← 34 feet →

Window Washer Level

Upper Mechanical Level

35th Floor

34th Floor

33rd Floor

32nd Floor

31st Floor

30th Floor

Detail of Tower Pediment—East Elevation

8th thru 29th Floor

1   2   3   4   5   6   7   8   9   10

7th Floor

6th Floor

5th Floor

feet

Mechanical Level

Dining Level

Sky Lobby

feet

Pit Level

feet

Lobby

Short Flat Arch   *Tall Flat Arches*   **F** *Main Arch*   *Tall Flat Arches*   *Short Flat Arch*

His theory was that the modular and the structural sense of Gothic is modern. And in a way, the whole transfer to steel was a Gothic thought. But on the other hand, the look of Schinkel and Soane is very, very classical.

But if you're looking through The International Style's *images, there are a striking number of things that are off center. Do you see that as a tension?*

Well, Mies and I were much more classical than most. But don't forget the Greek aspects of de Stijl. Mies published in his magazine *G* lots of things from the de Stijl group. But you see, architects are blind when it comes to influences.

There are critics who are uncomfortable with your work because they see the transformation of your style over time. That you moved from the modern to other idioms is troubling for them. How would you respond to the people who are ideological about modernism's correctness?

I have a hard time. Because if they start with that *parti pris* – Giedion did – then nothing's going to change.

But from day one, you saw modernism for its design purposes?

Only. Because I came from history, along with Alfred Barr and Russell Hitchcock.

And modernism is simply part of the continuum?

Of course.

Where did postmodernism come from? Was it an outgrowth of the preservation movement?

If it hadn't been for the preservationist lobby, I don't think postmodernism would have got such a big start. I, as a historian, and Alfred Barr, as an academic, found the preservation cause appealing. We had an interest in looking at old buildings and trying to hang onto them. I think that tended to direct our minds towards what would later be called postmodernism.

On the other hand, we were getting bored with the box. There's no doubt about that. And we were interested in keeping our eyes open for various great periods. Of course, my interest in historical things also comes in. When I was 13, I was introduced to Gothic at the cathedrals in France, and they made an indelible impression. And the same thing happened in Greece when my mother kept taking me around. I always looked at the architecture. So it was a natural fit for me.

The term "postmodern" comes from Bob Stern, who is the most brilliant writer there is on historical things. It seemed natural when Stern was talking about this. I had done this sort of thing with Alfred Barr – we tried to save Penn Station. So it all brought

up memories and desires that were latent in my work with modern architecture.

You see, Mies and that generation came in only by thumbing their noses at history. But I came in through history, and that's exactly opposite to the way most modern architects came in. So I embraced it the way I do everything; twice as hard as anybody else. I've always done that – more papal than the pope. I fell hard and fast. I wasn't a form giver like Mies. I wasn't making new shapes. I wasn't breaking new ground in my own architecture. I was pretty much a Mies pupil, so it was easier for me as a less-than-vastly-original young architect to be seduced, as it were, by new directions. I still am. I change very quickly. And when I saw what the kids – they are all kids to me – like Robert Stern and Michael Graves were doing, I was very proud of that as a new direction. They are both brilliant guys.

I had my own interest in history, which others shared. They had been educated the way I had, through history courses. I suspect that it's due to a lack of originality on my part that I grasped at a way to reintroduce history – I've never said this before, but I think it's part of this. I was looking for a haven, a way to use my knowledge of history. Then I also felt that it was happening anyhow. You take the Paolo Portoghesi direction in Italy. You take the

I was pretty much a Mies pupil, so it was easier for me as a less-than-vastly-original young architect to be seduced, as it were, by new directions.

movement in England that ended up with Prince Charles, the populism end. Postmodernism would be more popular than anything modern. This would be the way to go.

And then later, long after the AT&T Building, I started studying that building and realized what I had been missing. For instance, I used cushioned capitals in the lobby there. Well, a cushioned capital is a Romanesque device of the year, let's say, 1100, and there are very fine examples of it all over France. So what's it doing in that skyscraper?

It is the details, you see, and I can't work them all out, in spite of knowing my Brunelleschi. You wouldn't take any of his entrances and stretch them out that way with a great big arch and the lesser colonnade. Because the entrance to the AT&T Building is Brunelleschi's Pazzi Chapel. But it ain't, you see. I was trying to apply things that didn't fit. The Pazzi Chapel doesn't fit with a perfect cushioned column. I wanted to mix them up. I still don't mind that, because it's what you do with the classical that is important – how you twist it. But that had been done better by the mannerists of the sixteenth century. I realized that I just didn't

FILIPPO BRUNELLESCHI'S PAZZI CHAPEL

understand the basic rhythms that Charles Follen McKim under-stood somehow. Because there was his University Club on Fifth Avenue in New York, and that is a perfect example of how you can use Florentine examples and still do it right. I wasn't doing it right and neither are the other postmodernists. I don't know who in the postmodern gang can do it right.

You don't think you did it right in the Boston Public Library addition next to McKim's original?

But that wasn't really postmodern. I wasn't trying to be a classicist. A great deal of the classical is the module, you see, which I deliberately destroyed and made modern there. I think the ideological reasoning behind that wing is better than the ideological backing to postmodernism. That would have been clear to me at the time I was doing AT&T, if I had looked at it. In fact, that's what Hitchcock's criticism of my wing always was, that I had lost the scale, which was the main point of the Renaissance. And that was gone. I said that was fine because I wanted to do a nine-square building, which is classical enough, but I kept the nine squares as the expression and did not try to put a facade on it. In other words, the nine squares were represented in all three facades.

The three arches that you developed on that building seemed almost to be the result of doing a closeup shot of the entrance to the original library building and then enlarging it 500 percent.

The roof line is the same as the original building, as is the cornice. I would defend the BPL addition almost more than I can de-fend some of my more postmodern work. Although, my latest one was the best – the MTR, the Museum of Television and Radio. There, I understood one thing: in New York if you did a deconstructivist building on a long road of six-story buildings and you made it 17 stories high, it would look wrong – it would jar. So I wanted to join it with the city *Stadtbild*, the city picture.

Paul Goldberger criticized the MTR entrance as a throwaway. It was. It's a piece of the familiar form, and I see nothing wrong with that even now. But of course, the building is more Gothic than classical. Well, what is it really, you see? It's a lot of nothing. It's Goodhue Gothic. But marvelously, what it does do is to make an accent on the street without disturbing it. I mean you can have the older restaurant, the 21 Club, right next to it, and it's quite mild and nice, which I think it should be. See, there are some rules you should follow when building in the city. I am working on this in Berlin now. There are things that you shouldn't do. This site was no place to try modern post-deconstructivist shapes.

So in essence, it's more of a good citizen.

That's right. I was trying to be a good citizen, and I think we've succeeded. I think the white stone is beautiful. Bill Paley, the patron of the building, picked it out. Actually, you never see the top of the MTR. How would you ever do that? You would have to take down about ten buildings to get that view. It's top heavy if you see the whole thing. But in reality, I think, it looks all right. I'm pleased with it.

It almost looks like a glazed terra cotta from far away.

Yes, it's all right, but when you see that it's stone, it's a very nice feeling. So I don't know. Postmodern has so many different tones. I mean how rigid are you going to be? How interpretative? And where's it going to go? Now all I know is that my own interest has changed.

There is a tendency in criticism to lump everything that came after Mies van der Rohe together as postmodernism. Moreover, anything that is "contextual" is called postmodern. Do you think that this definition is incorrect?

In truth, it's simpleminded, but it's natural. You lump things together and it makes it easier. For example, lots of people consider the Boston Public Library addition a postmodern work. Well, it hadn't been thought of like that when I was working on it in the 1960s.

Later, when Bob Stern and I were discussing how we were working, he said, "What it is is 'postmodern,' Philip." So we all glommed onto it, and it's been used ever since. But it's silly and it came on, like everything new, very gradually. It's like the start of Ledoux and Boullée and all those people under Louis XVI who became known as the "revolutionary architects." Why? They weren't revolutionaries in any sense.

It's the same with the Russian constructivists. They did their best work from 1914 to 1918, not in any revolutionary period. And yet there is a connection made between them and the revolution. It's just that the dates are too close – same as with Boullée and Ledoux – so it's too obvious to ignore. Still, the dating is very strange. Politics comes after art, yes. But are they really revolutionary? I think probably if you could have talked to Ledoux, you would have found he was just as proud of the palaces he built for the aristocracy as he was of all the sketches he did later. It's hard to say.

There tend to be two separate strains within postmodernism. There's historic revival, but there's also contextualism, and they don't necessarily go hand in hand. Do you think one is more important than the other?

I think the stomach takes over again; it doesn't go into words. Contextualism was a big part. Using classical forms was a big part. Contextualism was fine for the Boston Public Library, but classical forms? Hardly at all, you see, because that particular mixture of modern and contextualism was not postmodern.

On the other hand, that architect from New Haven, Allan Greenberg, does classical work. Is he postmodern? No, he's a classicist, you see. He wouldn't do a Gothic building. That's revivalism, surely, not postmodernism.

One of the best postmodern buildings is that woman's prison by Spaeth in Würzburg, Germany. There is a building that used classical in very peculiar ways – it was more "post-Ledoux" than anything. But I got revivalist too. Don't forget the Ledoux building I did for the University of Houston School of Architecture.

So what separates revivalism from true postmodernism?

You have to be original. Ledoux didn't copy Ledoux or anybody else. That was the building where I learned mostly what not to do. I somehow missed at the entrance there; I missed the sense of what Ledoux was doing. I got the idea of the top fine, that belvedere. It just *makes* the campus. I had to go to neoclassicism to make a campus. Naturally, that's what I was doing. So I don't say it was right or wrong, I just say that it didn't satisfy me.

But these dreams get mixed up and divided. What we really meant in emphasizing the postmodern was that we were getting away from stereotypes. After all, the International Style, as I have pointed out a hundred times, was a very, very long style, from 1920 to that dribble end of my own Glass House, 1950. Thirty years. The Renaissance wasn't that long. So I think it was overdue, the reaction against the modern style, more than anything.

It seems that now the reactions come faster.

I don't know if I am right or not, but it is like the river delta description in my 1970s speech in Dallas. Water can go canalized or it can all spread out the minute you get into flatland. And the Mis-

sissippi delta is extremely wide. So we're now all over the place. Same water. I mean, it all comes down to the sea, but you see it rushing in Minneapolis. It doesn't rush in Louisiana. It's just different, though it's the same water. It's interesting.

What should postmodernism do? Well, it should do what my Museum of Television and Radio did. It should do what the Würzburg prison did. You pick and choose. I think that Richardson was probably the best postmodernist, not in his Romanesque-

Richardson was probably the best postmodernist, not in his Romanesque-looking buildings, but in the Marshall Field wholesale store.

looking buildings, but in the Marshall Field wholesale store. For instance, when Frank Lloyd Wright went classical, he went "classical" classical. Like his design for the museum in Milwaukee with its classical colonnade. Then he did the Moore House, an interesting Gothic house. That's why I would defend my Ledoux imitation in Houston.

Well, what the client wanted always plays an enormous part. But all these different things get all mixed up, don't they? Of course, today, then, we end up nowhere. A little contextualism, a little deconstructivism.

As you say, we're across the map.

The design I am now producing for an office building in Berlin, Das Business Center – as opposed to the design I'd like to do – is sort of a 1914 street pattern, because that fit what the city wanted. They have every right to say what they want. But this seemed kind of sad to me when the context of the site was just a rock. There was nothing to really fit in with. It's just a trace in the middle of a desert. So they could have had anything they wanted. They chose to reproduce the street pattern and the cornice line and make the street the composition. Of course, they have the right to do that.

But you think that was an error on their part?

I certainly do, and I said so in my speech that I gave in Berlin in 1993. I say that you've got to have something of our time. So just for fun, I designed a different building. It's a pretty violent form, and they're going to die when they see it, I hope.

You say that a building has to have something from the period in which it's created, and yet you do believe in contextualism.

If you started a *new* contextualism with my building, why not?

Do you have a favorite spot in New York City?

I keep getting asked that question. The garden at The Museum of Modern Art. I suppose urbanistically the best is the plaza at 59th Street and Fifth Avenue – ruined by Mr. Ed Stone by trying to make another plaza on the Plaza plaza. He should have put *that* plaza on Madison Avenue. If he had just reversed it! Then he'd have created another city picture back there.

Don't you have to step up two steps to that plaza too?

Oh yes, you step up, but mostly you fall in a hole. That sort of arrangement didn't work at Rockefeller Center and doesn't work here either.

Mies's reaction to Rockefeller Center was, and I agreed, "Philip, it's pretty much all right because if the field is big enough and if there are enough daisies in it, then it's all right." I never liked it because I always saw what I would do with it. I was never fair. But I liked what Hood did on his own.

They gave the designers of Rockefeller Center each a weekend: "Now boys it's time to stop all this bickering. You go off and spend a weekend and bring us back what you would like to do with this." And what Hood did was take the roads and then cross them in an X and put four great buildings on the X. Brilliant idea. But the way it came out is a compromise, like Lincoln Center.

H. H. RICHARDSON'S MARSHALL FIELD AND COMPANY WHOLESALE STORE

Was urban design and planning a long-term interest of yours?

Always. About 1928 I started thinking about it, and then later on I read Choisy and how he described the Acropolis. There are two great places, of course, San Marco Square in Venice and the Acropolis in Athens. They're opposites – one's up, one's down, same thing. And then I read the medieval plans from Sitte. So if you read Sitte and Choisy, you really can't help being interested in city planning.

And you read this back when you were first studying in the 1920s?

Oh, yes. I studied that in 1928 and 1929. I remember a lecture once on Haarlem. The lecture discussed how you walk up to a square, at an angle, and discover the square. You turn angles as you enter the square, which is dominated by a town hall or a cathedral. But you can't see anything directly. It's the opposite of the baroque. You can't see straight lines running off here. All you see are walls, because the streets all come together.

I've always been interested in planning. The greatest plan in the world, of course, is the Ryōanji Garden of Kyoto, which is a temple court with great rocks floating in the sand. That's a city plan. So is the museum garden at MoMA. You come in and your

I've gotten looser. My latest thing in Berlin and my visitors pavilion in the country – with their wave forms – they're as antifunctionalist as you can get.

circulation is compelled by those four different sides and the open rooms.

The idea of being contained has always fascinated me. That's why I tried to make a containment out of Lincoln Center. I tried to close the front and make a court.

Can you describe how you go about designing a building?

You start backwards. I'm a Harvard man, therefore I'm a functionalist, and I cannot get it out of my system.

But you're trying?

Oh, of course. Who wants to look like a Harvard man, or a Gropius man?

I want to call it the Harvard Architectural School, instead of the Harvard Graduate School of Design. I told the school I'd be back as soon as they changed the name. I'm famous for that.

So you're a Harvard man, therefore you're . . .

Therefore I'm a functionalist, and as a functionalist I always start with the kitchen and the plumbing. I don't back up to plumbing, necessarily. But that functionalist approach was so ingrained in the Bauhaus method that there was no escaping it. Of course, with Mies, I got to be a formalist, all right. But recently, I've gotten looser. My latest thing in Berlin and my new visitors pavilion in the country – all the waves – they're as antifunctionalist as you can get. I tried to put a door on my little building in the country. Couldn't. A door looks perfectly absurd. It looks perfectly right in the drawing, you see. But you can't do that in the third dimension.

Well, I did it. Look, every airplane has a door; that's the design process. It's backwards and upside down, and it works mainly when you're talking to somebody else, or when you're in the shower or walking down the street. It rarely happens to me with a pencil in my hand.

Does it ever happen at night?

No. It usually happens on the walk between my library and my house. That's about a three-minute walk. I may be frustrated, after having been screaming at pieces of paper all day in the library. Then as I walk to tea – I make a break for tea in the country – something happens. I don't know where it comes from; it doesn't come from anywhere. I don't sit down and design something.

I am an exception here, because I also look at other people's work. Frank Stella did an architectural job for Dresden. I had a model lying around in the studio. So when I showed my new building to Stella, he said, "Oh, Dresden Two." All right, if he thinks that. Gehry says it's pure Stella, and Stella says it's pure Eisenman. I don't know what it is. But we're all in the same loose sort of a boat.

The most important man in my horizon right now is a man named Hermann Finsterlin; he's the new guru. Finsterlin was exactly the same age as Mies, absolutely contemporary. And he built only one house. He was a very late expressionist. But Mies was also an expressionist, only he liked straight lines more. The plan of that glass skyscraper – I mean, where did Mies get that? No, Mies was an original sort of a guy, and he was influenced by the funniest things.

How do you pass your ideas on to your coworkers?

I give them drawings and sketches that I've done. But I have people who understand. John Manley has been with me for 38 years. He does the drawings better. I don't draw.

We don't picture you sitting with a T-square.

No, I can't use one. I don't have one, not in the country, where I do my so-called thinking. But thinking comes at the funniest times. I think everybody would say the same thing. Not everybody uses models as much as I do. There are original architects, like Mies, who don't have to look at anything.

So you find models more useful for developing ideas?

Well, the idea first goes into a drawing, then into a model, and then back. It's a much longer process.

For example, there were four or five different floor plans for the Glass House, weren't there?

Sixteen.

You were Mies's assistant on the Seagram building. How did its famous restaurant, the Four Seasons, come about?

We had this empty space — we didn't know it was going to be a restaurant. So we thought, "Well, it's going to be a Cadillac showroom." And then Phyllis Lambert said, "Look, what are we going to do in this space?" A restaurant couldn't pay the rent for the space; it was not on the ground floor. You couldn't make it a shop; that would be inappropriate. So Mr. Bronfman and Phyllis decided that the space should be subsidized.

When was it decided that you, not Mies, would do the interiors for the Four Seasons?

Oh, Mies got tired. "For God's sake, I don't want to sit here and do a restaurant. You do it." He wanted to go back to Chicago. That's where his girlfriend, and life, were.

Did you have doubts about doing an interior?

I should say not! It was the Seagram Building. But I wouldn't do it again; no more restaurants.

Restaurants are very tricky. And usually, there's never enough money. But there was here. That was the cheapest way we could use that space. Of course, no restaurant would have done what we did — it would have been tinsel. The Four Seasons, now that is architecture.

That interior is now landmarked, isn't it?

It's landmarked, and the owners of the building hate that.

Do you typically think about the exterior of the building first and then the interior, or are both of equal importance?

It all depends on what you start with. Some of my buildings are exterior buildings, and some are interior. The Museum of Television and Radio is an exterior building, because inside what can you do? I built a lot of buildings like that. There are no interiors in them, although it's all very classical. There's no spatial feeling of any kind. There can't be in a little tiny thing like that. Also, it is designed not for seeing art on the wall but for watching television, listening to radio, or watching a movie. Movies especially are anti-spatial. Oh, television is a great enemy of architecture. Not as bad as elevators though.

How do you see the media affecting architecture?

It's just part of the same ending of architecture. If you're going to sit and look at the boob tube, you can't see architecture at all. You just don't even look up. You know, it takes a little eye training. And yet, look at the Renaissance — they were not educated.

The Museum of Television and Radio is an exterior building, because inside what can you do? I built a lot of buildings like that.

How the hell did they get the money or resources to build those incredible monuments, and who liked them? And why?

And they were popular.

Were they? They were popular because they were big.

Also, there was not a lot of other competing visual interest, so of course, you'd find the Piazza San Marco entertaining.

Well, my theory on the idea of the piazza is that you have to consider the way it's used. Every town in Italy closes up about 6 P.M. because the people have to walk in the public square. And they go around counter-clockwise. Then all of a sudden, as if there's a signal, gone. Now those people do that through their social structure. We don't have a social life any more because the boob tube has settled that.

The other thing that makes the square is the fact that people live in such squalor. Have you ever stayed over night on one of those streets in back, about ten blocks from the Piazza San Marco? If you have, then you know how good the piazza looks. But if you stay at the Gritti Palace Hotel, you'll never know how good the piazza is. People coming from those little streets are squeezed, like out of a tube. I mean, they've got to go to the piazza. That's their newspaper, their television, their everything. It is life in that square.

What is the reaction of the people? Again, you can feel it in the stomach, you feel it by the way they promenade. Why they prom-

enade in that way I don't know, but people are funny. They do that at the Opera in Paris. They won't do it here. We gave them a perfect place to do it, and they won't. I did the State Theater for that. Americans won't promenade like that. Because they've lost any sense of community.

Churches were the same way back then. What incredible entertainment value, with mosaics and paintings, incense and hoopla.

Yes, and then they carried it right out into the plaza on those six-feet high stages – they were correctly six feet. I have never come across anybody who makes a podium in a square in this country high enough. Yet any medieval stage was six-feet high. So you can watch what is happening from a flat floor from the plaza. Today they put a three-foot podium out for people to talk from. Nobody can see the speaker. It doesn't make any sense.

Do details interest you as much as the overall form of the building? Or do you delegate them to other people?

Oh, you should never delegate. You try to, but they don't understand detail.

I've been at it three years in Berlin. They didn't like my corner, my window. They said it wasn't strong enough, or something. So I've been doing the detail of that corner off and on for about three

The statues on the roof of 580 California were a throwback to seventeenth- and eighteenth-century sculpture that is integrated into the building.

years. I solved it, finally. What do they mean, not strong enough? Of course it's strong enough. But I'm apt to argue, you see. That takes time and energy. Three men out there can't do it right. But not John Manley, he always does it right.

Did you get involved with all the details in the AT&T Building?

Oh, sure, every one. But some of them are not as good as others. I should have had more full-scale mock-ups. I did it at Dumbarton Oaks. That's what every architect should use. Of course, most can't afford to do full-scale mock-ups. But Mrs. Bliss, my client down at Dumbarton Oaks, not only could afford it but demanded it. So we built a whole unit – there are nine units in that design – in a big room that she had in her big place. We went over every single one of the details, every piece of the bronze. We got the actual wood that we were going to use in the tapered floor, and the

column, and we mocked it up. We wanted to study how that proportion would look in real life. She and I sat there and then changed things and worked on it. It helped the design.

Speaking of details, how did you come up with the draped statues on top of 580 California Street in San Francisco?

The statues, of course, on the roof of 580 California were a definite throwback to seventeenth- and eighteenth-century sculpture that is integrated into the building. We don't integrate anymore. Today we have a free-standing statue against a background. So I said, well if they could do it in the seventeenth century, let's take a sculpture and do the same. The sculptor, Muriel Castanis, was doing these very monumental Greek things, but with the faces omitted, just hollow. I thought this was the kind of thing that should go up there. So we put them in. In actuality, I'm not sure that was a wise move. I'm not sure that we really got the effect that we dreamed of in our minds. It was a nice idea. But the idea was to integrate the sculpture into the building in ways more similar to the old than the new.

The new way of integrating was, of course, what Mies did at Barcelona, an Alexander Calder sculpture standing free with a travertine wall behind it. But in this case, I wanted to crown the vertical piers of the building with these statues. And it's amusing. But maybe the building's too tall. Maybe you can't do it by isolating them. Maybe they have to be integrated as they are in French beaux-arts with the actual background of the decorative scheme. But we're in a different world from the eighteenth century. It may be that we shouldn't even try.

Your details, such as the lighting fixtures in International Place in Boston, were so distinctive in the 1980s. How did you decide on these? Those chandeliers seem so out of scale, so fun yet elegant.

The lighting fixtures were a great passion of mine because I like to change scale with them. In Boston, they were used to call attention to the centering of a room. That room was amorphous. It was part of a circle, but it didn't have a regular shape. So to point it up and give it an idea that that was a room of some importance, I used the chandeliers to add elegance. At that time, I didn't know where to go for a good chandelier. So we found this firm out in Salt Lake City that specialized in that kind of work. So I can't say that the design was mine. It was theirs. There's so much work in a chandelier that designing one is outside the field for most of us. So that detail is a stranger there. But it did do that particular thing that I wanted, which was to call attention to a room, in the middle of a skyscraper lobby. And it did that. I apologize for the fact that I didn't actually design it. I would need another lifetime, it seems to me, to design a chandelier.

The other thing it brought in was a reminiscence of the seventeenth and eighteenth centuries. It is an allusion, ironic though it may be, to another century where elegant rooms had chandeliers. They are familiar objects. So I kept using the chandelier.

There is the sheer scale of them; that wasn't danger so much as the fun of it. It was the idea, not the design, because to me we don't live in a design age.

We're not interested in design the way people were in past ages. Our energies are not dedicated to that. Our crafts are not nearly as good as they were in the arts and crafts period, of 1910, the period when Frank Lloyd Wright did his good furniture. It became lousy toward the end in the forties and fifties.

The lighting fixtures were a great passion of mine because I like to change scale with them. In Boston, they call attention to the centering of a room.

But even Wright's early chairs were never comfortable. They were not meant to be comfortable, any more than Mies's were. Try and sit in them. In my house, the only two chairs that are never sat in are the Barcelona chairs. The best chair today is the Frank Gehry chair, which I have both in my office as well as in the studio in the country.

We're no longer in the great design age – like the art nouveau and the art deco. The French designers were truly marvelous, but they were the end of the line. I mean, modern design has never turned up anyone.

So given that, you have to look to other design eras?

You look to other periods if you want to get something funny or something out of scale or something outrageous.

That's a pop sensibility.

No, pop is wrong. I am a very serious architect. I adore Warhol; he was a great friend of mine, and he was certainly pop. But that is part of the low-high art business – that the low art can become high art through people like Warhol. But I'm not after low art. There's nothing low art about hanging a chandelier that is the wrong scale around. That's a recall of other centuries that has resonances in the back of your mind. Well, pop does too. Pop takes an image of Marilyn, or Popeye the Sailorman, as a thing which can be recalled and amusing too. For my work, irony is a better word, or fun, or humor, or something even more serious. It is like my saying that I use chandeliers because it's an elegant symbol of a long-past era that I like. That isn't a pop sensibility. So people that call my work pop are just plain – don't know pop. Because pop is a very definite, very interesting style of painting of the 1960s and 1970s.

So what would be the source of your manner of using irony and humor in architecture?

You could say that it has a relationship with the Duchampian approach to irony. Although I think in my case you will find that any allusions are historic. I make attempts to pick historic objects or juxtapositions that work in new ways. It's like the statues at 580 in California. The attempt was brave, and sometimes successful, other times less so. That's bound to be the case if you're an artist who wants to do offbeat things that sometimes don't quite do what one thinks they would have done. But that's okay with me. That comes with the territory.

At International Place in Boston, you use the Palladian window ad infinitum. Was that the conception? Were you having a little fun there?

Have fun, always try to get fun in. I like to use traditional things in a fairly odd way. That is one famous thing that people get me for, as it were, the Palladian windows in International Place. But I would just merely say, "Why not?" I mean, they put windows that they get from the eighteenth century all over buildings all the time. Nobody thinks that's funny. I think Palladian windows have a rather prettier shape. I wasn't trying to make any more important point than that. It is like a dot pattern. There is such a thing as an ordinary dot, and there is also a more amusing dot. So I say, if you're going to have lots of dots, let's have an amusing one. And that was all there was to that.

Can you explain your use of that attenuated arch that's at the center of 500 Boylston, and also in Tycon Towers in Virginia and the

I think Palladian windows have a rather prettier shape. I wasn't trying to make any more important point than that. It is like a dot pattern.

M Bank [formerly Momentum Place] in Dallas? Where did that come from?

I think my use of it was a simple reference to the beaux-arts period. I think you can see the beginnings of it in the AT&T Building. There the fenestration changes abruptly in the middle and makes a centralized opening. I got the round top from another reference. All over New York are these buildings that have bent sheet metal ceilings and that have a Palladian window entrance as a basic theme.

FIVE HUNDRED BOYLSTON

Do you feel that because the second tower at 500 Boylston Street was not built, you lose even more than 50 percent?

Putting it as a percentage – that's pretty good. I thought we had lost 60 percent. But it is too high for its proportions.

If you could do it over again, would you still use that arch?

Well, I wouldn't do the project, let's say that. I don't want to break a building in two, anyhow. What I do like is the individual floor, which John Burgee used over at Takashimaya. And I like the base and I like the court – even though the proportions aren't quite right.

Paul Goldberger said in 1986 that your architecture is about other architecture more than a pure work of art itself. How do you feel about that?

I resent it, but I understand what he means. I don't think people copy, or adapt, or whatever you want to say, quite as much as I do. But how can you be more Miesian than my house? And yet it is different.

They just don't do it as openly as you.

And they're not willing to admit it. Well, I have a peculiar approach to history, no doubt about it, and I use it a lot more. Eisenman, for instance, knows his history perfectly, but he wouldn't think of using it.

Recently I had some students come to the house. And we talked for a couple of hours. Exhausting, but I enjoyed it. I tried to drag out of them where their inspirations come from, but they couldn't tell me. I told them that it was impossible not to have influences. So what architects do they like to look at? I reduced it to that. They told me "Venturi." I said, "Don't you like Gehry? What about Le Corbusier?" No, nothing like that. When I asked, "Why?" that was fatal, because they answered, "Because his buildings are very socially minded." About Venturi! I said, "You go home and go sit in a corner."

What do you think of the modernist sensibility that rejects history, that architectural form always has to be a new development?

That's ridiculous. They say that, but Eisenman went way beyond that.

Do you think that if you put more effort into being less clear, to couch what you say in more high falutin academic language, then the critics would take you more seriously? Or is it your sense of humor that throws them off?

No, I think it's a problem because it's true. I don't think I am a big time original architect. I'm no Frank Gehry; I'm different. I think everybody has said bad things about me, and they're usually right. But they don't bother me.

I'm not an intellectual in their sense of the word. I may be bright enough, no way I can tell. But if something occurs to me, I say it. And other people, I think, ratiocinate a little more. They think. I don't. I react. Well, that's a good or a bad trait, you see. But it gets me into trouble all the time. But it's the trouble that makes people want to write about it, and I think it sometimes sounds simply terrible. Like saying Frank Lloyd Wright is the greatest architect of the nineteenth century. With that I was both right and wrong. It's rather a good statement. But it's flip.

But some people, who probably should know your work better than they do, will discount it and say, "Well, you know, it's not really that serious."

"He's always playing a joke, he's always laughing at the world." Well, I see my work in a sequence of history, and I see no

I see my work in a sequence of history, and I see no contradiction between that and modern. I mean, architecture is always a revolution.

contradiction between that and modern. I mean, architecture is always a revolution. My new expressionist period doesn't connect with modern but there's enough of a relationship there. A few years ago, historic images were my big god. But images change and you go on. How boring to make the same building this year you did last year.

Mies is a bore. But when Mies was doing a single building, oh boy. And those four that he did in 1920, 1921, 1922 – the ones that he never built – are the greatest and most different buildings imaginable. The point of the skyscraper – the curve! Then he got into a set style. Mies never talked about history. He used the word, of course. You see he had two great historical backgrounds: the Catholic church and Schinkel. He was very Catholic, Rhineland Catholic. Gropius was Prussian.

Was Mies interested in Viollet-le-Duc?

Oh, no. His interest in the Gothic really was through Thomas Aquinas, his pseudo-philosophy.

At the time of the International Style show at The Museum of Modern Art, did you feel that this was the true and only style? Would you say that you were a true believer?

A true believer, sure. But the functionalist part and the Marxian part left me cold, because to me architecture is a pure art, and it's art that interests me. People accuse me of that, and say that's wrong. But art is the main point of architecture. "What about sociology? What about the people? Don't you care about people at all?" The answer is "no," of course. I mean I respect the scale of a human being, but the people themselves? What have they got to do with architecture? It's how to make people feel. If you feel good

To me, Plato was the worst – living the good and the true. There's no such thing. I'm a relativist. I'm a nihilist.

or feel uplifted, that's what I'm aiming at. Anybody who comes to any building of mine and starts getting tears in his eyes, you've got me for life. But that's the aim, not the bathrooms. People did very well without bathrooms, but they have never done well without architecture.

You are known for defending architecture as an art. What about the social content of architecture?

The social content of architecture is very important. Though the particular work I'm in hasn't got that social dimension. It's more sculpture.

But you did have work that had the social dimension, when you did master plans.

Oh, I'm very interested in that. I mean, what architect wouldn't want to build a city? It's only the greatest challenge in the world! One of my old saws that I've used so much is: "The hardest things in the world are stairs, chairs, and public squares." That's my oldest one. But it is the truth. I still cannot do stairs. I'm still working on them.

Your stairs at the New York State Theater are pretty successful.

They are. And that was the hardest part. I think I spent more time mocking them up, and making the corners so you'd come up easily. That's very, very important. But the point is: stairs are hard. And chairs – I've done enough to know. My best chairs fall down when a heavy man teeters back in them. My worst one was so low I could never get out of it myself, although I was quite young. The Barrs [Alfred Barr and his wife] had it in their living room until the end. A sling chair with a Miesian frame. So I realized I was lousy. That's why I'm all the more admiring of Gehry. That chair of his I think is wonderful. It's bouncy, and yet you can

move around in it. You can tilt back in it, all those things you naturally do in a chair.

Designing decorative objects and furniture doesn't appeal to you?

No, those things do appeal to me. I've done salt shakers. I've done watches.

You've done watches?

Well, I did one for my sister, through Cartier. Cartier didn't have anything to do in 1932. For $125 I designed a watch. But even then it was difficult. Oh, I had lots of fun. But it took a long, long time. I also did a satin dress for her. I did these things because I hadn't had any training as an architect, and I thought that was very important – to get training. That was before I knew better. The salt cellars I did were just cylinders.

It was all in the 1930s, before I went to school. I didn't realize you'd have to know something about design in order to design anything, you see. No matter how you learn it. I don't care if you learn it just by hit or miss, over the years. But when I was young, I was never conscious enough to sit down and think that way about design. It took architecture to get me to do that. And Mies. Somehow, it's got to come. It can come in the shower, or on a walk. But you have to have your main brain on it. You can't go reading Tolstoy or attending concerts when you design.

Do you enjoy other art forms, like music and dance?

I *enjoy* music very much. I love early music, especially Renaissance music. Just before the baroque. That's a very strange little love to have, isn't it? But I wouldn't say I was fundamentally *interested* in music.

But dance? No, I don't understand dance at all. Kirstein can't understand my lack of interest in dance. Oh, Balanchine, that's different. But Balanchine is an architect. An architect that used human beings for shapes. Others use dance for expressing emotions. I'm sorry, I'd rather be in love. But Balanchine was cerebral – incomprehensibly brilliant. But his work is sculpture, architecture, and dance. He understood them all. He understood religion. He was the greatest artist – total artist – of our time.

Do you like to go to the opera?

Well I don't mind bathing in a little Puccini. Although, of course, Verdi was the great composer, people tell me. But I love *Turandot*, I'm sorry. I can bathe in that anytime.

If you're working, do you like to listen to music?

No, I do not. Music distracts me into the music. Mozart, for instance, is much too interesting to work with. And I don't want that distraction.

Well it's not an accident that we call architecture the mother of the arts, because it's so inclusive. I mean, the right place for a painting is – any architect can tell you – on a wall.

Does the same hold true for sculpture?

Well, depending on what you mean by sculpture. Not necessarily Brancusi. He's a thing in itself. Bernini, of course, was a sculptor and an architect. Though Borromini, of course, looked down on that use of sculpture as a crutch, because Borromini wasn't a sculptor. He resented Bernini because he didn't think of him as an architect.

Do you prefer Bernini to Borromini?

No, Borromini. Well, look, I love Bernini. Anybody who could conceive that square in front of St. Peter's . . .

Is it the sense of humor in Borromini that you like, his wit?

It is the wickedness.

How do you describe yourself philosophically?

My philosophical outlook dates from a time and a way of thinking that differs from the liberal, acceptable, politically correct line that we all subscribe to today. To me, Plato was the worst – living the good and the true and the beautiful. There's no such thing as the good or the true or the beautiful. I'm a relativist. I'm a nihilist. Well, it's a long background, one with a lot of history, and an honorable one.

I learned the German language, when I was young, because I was interested in reading Nietzsche. And I still read Nietzsche, in German, because it's much better. He's a poet and a thinker. That's why I was initially attracted to Hitler, who totally misunderstood Nietzsche, really. But there was enough similarity between them so I got very excited about it. That was long before the problems for the Jews came up. It all ended in the frightful war, so of course, it was wrong.

How does art fit into that attitude?

Art, of course – Nietzsche said it – is the most important thing in the world. Art is with us in order that we not perish from the truth – if you understand truth as he did. Nietzsche felt that art is more important than philosophy. The hierarchy of important things in the world starts with art, not with looking for truth, or science, or anything. Well, that naturally appeals to artists. And, of course, the "will to power" sounds like a horrible term, but that's what will to power means. Will to power means, "How can I do the best art in the world?" Nietzsche's image got all warped because of Hitler. And of course, Nietzsche came long before him and wouldn't have approved of him at all.

The media have made your remark in Charlottesville, "I am a whore and I am paid very well for building high-rise buildings," a signature line for you. Was that something that just came off the top of your head?

Oh, yes.

Wasn't it just a little premeditated? Or were you simply having a little bit of fun?

No, no. You need to see that quotation in its context. You see, I just jumped up talking. But, of course, it made a wonderful quotation for people to attack. After all, any stick is good enough to beat a donkey with. The quotation was picked up by the *Boston Globe* architecture critic, Robert Campbell. "We don't want

Art – Nietzsche said – is the most important thing in the world. Art is with us in order that we not perish from the truth – if you understand truth as he did.

whores in Boston," was the headline. That's all right. I suppose that I opened myself up to it. Those words that Campbell put in my mouth were right. I did say them. But I said them like we're talking here. No, Campbell wanted to sell copy, and that is exactly what he did.

We are still curious why the majority of people are not more knowledgeable about the content of your work. What do you think is the explanation? Is it just that your quotations get in the way? Or are people jealous of your success?

No, not at all. I haven't had success. I have no work compared with a big architect. No, they're not jealous. It's just a dislike of chameleon-like publicity seekers. "He's just a publicity monger," that's all. "He says he's a whore because he thinks it's funny." I said a private and humorous thought. Well, I ought to have more sense.

Actually, I don't have any sense. But I'm still here. The trouble is that those comments take away from any interest people could have in the shapes I make.

People recognize your name, if nothing else.

My name recognition would be high.

On the Boards

DAS BUSINESS CENTER, BERLIN, GERMANY, ACCEPTED DESIGN

Philip Johnson works full-time from his Third Avenue office in New York. His current projects include some of the largest developments in Manhattan: the Times Square Redevelopment for Park Tower Realty, and Riverside South, a multi-block mixed-use project on the west side for Donald Trump. He is also working for the Central European Development Corporation on a Berlin office building – aptly called Das Business Center – near the former Checkpoint Charlie.

Johnson's current work reveals his latest direction in architecture, a far more sculptural, expressionistic style than his work of the 1980s. The building that embodies this artistic passion the most is the visitors pavilion he is building on his own property in New Canaan. As usual, Johnson will develop new ideas to their fullest extremes at the Glass House.

Hardly edging his way towards retirement, Johnson admits that he would consider packing up and moving to Rome when he turns 100. That won't happen until 2006. Until then commissions are being accepted.

What are the biggest obstacles you now face in architecture?

The problems I have now are the design restrictions applied to buildings in New York City. You should see what I'm up against at Riverside South. And in Times Square they're cutting all the tops off the buildings I designed. The city doesn't want them so high.

This sounds like the story of Pennzoil Place. You were told to cut the tops off on that project, which you did, and then you had to put them back.

But there I had a genius named Hugh Liedtke. Today, of course, it's a good market for those who oppose development, but a bad market for architects. I have nothing to stand on against the city.

And there's no Rockefeller to help you.

There's nobody. No mayor, no governor. What these towers will look like without those tops – well, that's just one instance. In Berlin it's entirely different. The city has rules in the part of the city where our site is. You have to have a cornice line of 22 meters. Then you have a mansard roof, or a setback, that can go to 30 meters. Now this means that you can't cut the building flat-topped. It means that you can't cut a hole in the plan and make a curved bay, and you can't have a tower sticking up to announce the building. It has to be a plain block that's 22 meters throughout the Friedrichstraße. That is a very low building for America, and I find it a very hard restriction to overcome when I am designing.

Now that was in the beginning. Then the client in Berlin wanted a glass building, because it should be *moderne*. Then they wanted an all-stone building because that was traditional. Then they wanted a variegated form, so it wouldn't be too boring; 280 feet of a straight-plane, ordinary facade is boring. So I had all of these constraints to work against, and I used, in the final plan, a sort of gable – one that can stick through the mansard out to the cornice line – and made these gables into the tops of towers. So I mixed towers with the mansard, but it really is the towers that you read. I tried to get some variety by making different thicknesses in the towers and by placing them randomly. Then I introduced a sloping plane of glass here and there. So I had towers alternating with all glass. I don't find it bad at all! I rather like it. But that's liking it within restrictions that make my teeth on edge all the time. So I fall between seven cracks and come up with the best I can. Let's say that. A mansard roof! I can't conceive of that in modern architecture.

Why is that?

Well, to go back to the old Hitchcock days in the 1930s, a mansard roof showed a sense of masonry and classicism of the nineteenth century that we were fighting against. I'm willing to tip the roof back. But I would tip the whole wall! A mansard is a no-no in modern architecture, that's all. But they – "they" in this case being the city fathers – wanted the Friedrichstraße to be as near to the way it was before as it could be. The Friedrichstraße was laid out in the eighteenth century. In those days, the buildings were all the same. They were boring – all the same height, only as high as you could walk up by foot. They had no elevators.

So it's logical, if you want to recreate the Friedrichstraße, to do it that way. And that's what I have often said. I never argue with a city that wants a particular part of their city to have a certain look. And yet, I can't help resenting it as an architect who wants to

The Friedrichstraße was laid out in the eighteenth century. In those days, the buildings were all the same. They were boring.

break new ground. My instincts are too strong for that. But I did discipline myself, and I got away with certain things. It will be a more interesting building than the others I'm working on, I think.

Toward the end I got so frustrated that I decided, just for fun, to design my own "fantasy Berlin" for the site. It turned out that it was very expressionist, and that it looked as if I had been looking at the work of Hermann Finsterlin – which indeed I had. The expressionist movement has been much maligned. But it really was a great forerunner of the modern. Mies, for instance, went through an expressionist period. All the great names that we know later as modernists were expressionists during those years of the late 1910s and early 1920s. The best-known example is Erich Mendel-

sohn's Einstein Tower. I am proud to be part of that. The buildings I designed for the fantasy use the same square footage, the same cubage, and the same lot as I had for the building they did build. So I enjoyed myself hugely, and I showed it in my lecture in Berlin: "In the meantime, I would have liked to have built this." And then I made no more comment, because it was clear I wasn't going to suggest it to anybody.

But you did show it to the client.

Yes, but he had no comment, of course.

What would the spaces be like inside your fantasy Berlin?

Very peculiar. Well, I learned – that ain't so bad. What do you think this is like to lay out? A nightmare! Every once in a while you can make a room, but as you get a little further along, somewhere you just give up. But I realized that if a building is interesting, you can usually make it work. Like the Lipstick building. There's a plus there because its shape is so peculiar. Everybody there has a corner room. These stupid arguments can be turned against naysayers. Peculiar is good.

I should call myself "the architect of these buildings based on sketches by Skidmore, Owings and Merrill." Because they don't come from me.

In some ways, the Berlin story and the Trump story at Riverside South in New York are similar. Mr. Trump, against his will and mine, has to build what the neighborhood and the city have dictated, and that is a retake of the art deco of Central Park West as designed by the firm Skidmore, Owings and Merrill. I often think I should call myself "the architect of these buildings based on sketches by SOM." Because they don't come from me. But I'm getting the same pleasure that I did in Berlin: "How can I squeeze out of these restrictions some fun and some interesting looks for the building?"

Nonetheless, you find it more pleasurable not to work under those restrictions?

Pleasurable? It isn't architecture at all! It's like doing a crossword puzzle. The rules are all laid out. "Page 33: the bay shall be 15 feet across." How much can you get away with? What can you really do in your struggle? I think the architect should have something to say. Someday I will write about it.

RIVERSIDE SOUTH, NEW YORK, RENDERING OF PRESENT VERSION

There are some architects who would say, "I like having those types of constraints, because it focuses my energies, and I'm solving a problem that is challenging."

It's really my eighth crutch, isn't it? [Johnson's speech "The Seven Crutches of Modern Architecture" was originally given at the Harvard University Graduate School of Design in 1954 and was later published.] I mean, the crutch of having so many requirements is that you just have to apply those instead of being original. But I rather like to do my own work.

The style that I have to use for the Trump project is based on the city code. It is sort of a semi-art deco, semi-*moderne* – as we used to call it – style that was really a classical style, influenced by the French Exposition of 1925. But it still was classical. In the early part of that period, Emery Roth was the leading hero, and he did some magnificent buildings, particularly the Cromwell apartment house on 72nd Street, just off Central Park West. Later on, other architects began to use corner windows, and stripped-down lines, and semi-ribbon windows – a little bit like Irwin Chanin's later things on Central Park West. The thinking behind that was that you could break up the city by putting double towers on the block, for instance. That kind of thing was considered a picturesque effect.

Well, as it happens, historically, that's where I came in during the thirties – in a wave of fury against the art deco. So it is especially ironic that I am now working under the restrictions of the art deco, as interpreted by the zoning lawmakers of 1990. They find it quaint and interesting and easy to copy, but it is very expensive, as I am now finding out.

To me, the art deco was a brief style. It lasted maybe four or five years and happened to have some very amusing towers, mainly descended from the great leader of it all, Emery Roth. But he was

It is especially ironic that I am now working under the restrictions of the art deco, as interpreted by the zoning lawmakers of 1990.

great, while many of the others were not. So in Riverside South, I was trying to pull back to Emery Roth's original ideas for twin towers. But I can't anymore, because the requirement of glass coverage has increased so violently. I can break a corner now and then and make a chamfered corner, though on the first three floors I have to have sharp corners. Sharp corners! Under the law, you can't do anything about it.

Why are you not allowed to chamfer the corners?

I don't know. Maybe because it doesn't use the full block, I think, or some interpretation of that. Now as sympathetic as I am to cities making their own rules to be more like the eighteenth century or 1930 art deco, the irony is too strong to be missed. For instance, my objection to the rules in Berlin is that there isn't anything eighteenth century within 50 miles of that part of Berlin. It's just inventing a memory that fits the particular inclinations of the current chairman of the city board. In New York it's the same way. The art deco was a very short period. It is interesting com-

I said, "I think balconies are awful." And Trump said, "Buzz, the balconies are out. We're not having any balconies in these buildings." At just that speed. Delicious.

pared with the brutal modern that everybody hates so much, that of the glass box. I can't help sympathizing with that. But to pick up and put into law the vagaries of a moment of such brevity as the art deco, I find that ironic.

Are you pleased to be doing something for Donald Trump?

I love him. He's as crazy as I am. He insisted on balconies, and I said, "I think balconies are awful." And he said: "Buzz, the balconies are out. We're not having any balconies in these buildings." At just that speed. Delicious. They don't care if he changes his mind. But I mean, that's kind of fun for people to talk that way.

The big problem in Riverside South, as I have mentioned, is that I'm restricted completely by the laws, which, nowadays, more and more design buildings for you. They don't give you any leeway for architectural work whatsoever. So here, the use of some object to decorate the tops of the building seemed to be the only thing to do. I looked in the loopholes of the law, and the only place I could find that was left to the architect was the top decoration, where the water tanks and the elevator overrides are. So I thought, Why don't we just pay no attention to the building downstairs and just put something on them that would make them look different? So I put an apple on top of one, the other a star, which fits everybody, the shape of the flame of the Statue of Liberty on the next, and finally, a heart. I don't know exactly why, but I expect a heart for New York. All of these objects that would be 50-feet high. I felt those symbols would be clear and could be read from across the river in New Jersey. However, after I thought about it, I decided it was just plain wrong. I didn't go ahead with it. It was just a reverie.

TIMES SQUARE REDEVELOPMENT, NEW YORK, DESIGN IN PRELIMINARY STAGE

TIMES SQUARE REDEVELOPMENT, NEW YORK, DESIGN IN PRELIMINARY STAGE

KING FAISAL FOUNDATION COMPETITION MODEL, SAUDI ARABIA

Did you ever consider putting a big slice of cheese on the top?

No, I did not. I did try to put a big "T" up there. But all of these objects ended up looking perfectly terrible. I mean, the relation of the top to its base was all wrong. I can imagine four pylons, with those four symbols, seen from across the river. But I can't imagine really building that way, and Mr. Trump thoroughly agreed. That was one day, one day in my thinking on that. It was fun.

When we were picking out things for the tops of buildings, one of the more amusing ideas was to put my glasses on it – about 50-feet high. I mean, a lot of pop ideas are very easy. Pop is something people strive for, something that they can identify with, or something they consider very funny. I assure you the apple looked very funny on top of these very serious art deco apartments by Skidmore, but I had to do something to their buildings!

What would you say to a critic who says, "But, it is funny looking. Are you not taking your work and audience seriously?"

Seriousness, irony, and humor I don't see as conflicting. I think the elements of danger and humor are very much a part of architecture. And symbolism is certainly a part. The apple represents the city. I'm perfectly serious.

If you were to have a clean slate to work with in the Riverside South project, how would you envision it?

What I hope to do is what I did in Berlin – make a building of the same size and requirements that would be new and different. Lots of things drift through my mind, like Frank Lloyd Wright's 1939 project for the Crystal Heights apartment towers in Washington, D.C. But I must say that right now I don't know, because I'm so involved in designing my way out of this 70-page book of requirements that I don't have time.

So is zoning ruining architecture?

Zoning is taking over architecture.

Hasn't that been going on for a long time?

Of course, but it hasn't always been a problem. One type of zoning allowed us to build the Seagram Building. The setback law of 1916 gave us the Gothic-style skyscrapers. If city planning is going to do that more and more – make design rules signed by a committee before the architect starts to work – it will prevent any new developments in design.

I think that the idea of using zoning to impose design is a little tough on architecture. They say, "Well, it's done in Washington." And I said, "No, it's not. There they zone for height." Washington is very much like Berlin in that respect. I built a building in Washington at 10 Franklin Square. You immediately think of the classical surroundings when you design for a site like that. It's

contextual, certainly. It never occurs to you not to be. But the rules in Washington allow for a broad range. They don't tell you the corner has to go "there."

So the city planning people are micro-managing it. They're getting too far into the details?

Well, they're designing. Nobody in Washington told me how to design. There, they just gave me the limits on height and density.

Is your reaction that it's just a bad idea to have design guideline commissions? You have certainly gone through this before in your work in Boston at 500 Boylston and International Place.

But those rules were no trouble. Those were normal restrictions: coverage, height, windows, and density.

But the second half of 500 Boylston wasn't built. Wasn't that due to the influence of design review?

No, that was the client, New England Life, that got mad at me.

The big debate surrounding design restrictions focuses on how to maintain the integrity of the city. What's your reaction to that?

Well, under that cloak, any clerk in any office can say, "I prefer this corner to that corner." Cities are trying to put into the law the points that Jane Jacobs made, but for exactly the opposite reason, some years ago. Her idea was the city just grows and has a flavor that you touch with great care. I mean, what you can't do is to go and build a modern building in the middle of Greenwich Village.

The city has every right to freeze Greenwich Village the way it is. But it's the variety in Greenwich Village that gives it its actual flavor.

Absolutely right. The city has every right to freeze Greenwich Village the way it is. But it's the variety in Greenwich Village that gives it its actual flavor. The same thing lower down in SoHo. Those are buildings that, by some luck, were built and remain today. The plots there are too small to assemble, in real estate terms. And if you can't assemble enough land, then you can't make a skyscraper. So fortunately, just by accident, the mid-rise, cast-iron buildings of SoHo have been preserved. But it's the people in those streets, and the little art galleries off them, including the buildings that are boarded up, that give SoHo its flavor. I can

KING FAISAL FOUNDATION COMPETITION MODEL, SAUDI ARABIA

– and do – have a nostalgia for that. But when you freeze the whimsical dictates of early – no, late – Emery Roth, it's another thing altogether.

Will the Times Square project be built anytime soon?

No. But the developer wants to keep dibs on the project because they've got a valuable license there. They've got $300 million already invested in it. Nobody wants to walk away from that at any cost.

You have been working on the redevelopment of Times Square for many years. How is the new scheme different?

The new one I like much, much better, of course. I never liked the big towers.

Then why did you do them originally?

Because I wanted a reminiscent thing that would look like the Pierre Hotel. I thought it would look natural. You have to have a top on these things. I was totally postmodern at that time, and I wanted to get that going. Bob Stern still likes it, better than the new one.

Do you think that project was instrumental in making you think about developing a new style?

No, those things happened separately. There was a lot of talk about a new way of looking at things and how classical was really a bore. What persuaded me most to go away from postmodern was that I couldn't get the detail. It just doesn't fit. I love those capitals I used at the AT&T Building, the cushioned Romanesque. But it's too disjointed to pick different elements for different parts of the building. The pediment, for example. People call it Chippendale. It wasn't really. It was Hadrianic. But those are bits and pieces you throw together.

It's more or less the same thing that people complained about in the teens, when the period revivals were so rampant. Thomas Tallmadge said something to the effect that everyone was pilfering the graves of history.

Well, that's what I have been doing. I don't mind pilfering anybody's grave, but I'd better do it in a consistent manner.

That's one of the criticisms that's been consistently thrown at you – that you use ideas from other architects, as though other architects don't do that.

Everybody does.

So it's just a question of how the models are used?

That's right. If you use everything with the greatest skill, it's fine. For example, Frank Lloyd Wright did a great beaux-arts museum for Milwaukee. Mies, of course was a wonderful classical architect. Brother! That Kröller-Müller project of 1912. What a house!

Even when you were working in a modern idiom, there's still something classical about your work.

Yes. In fact, there is a book that was published in 1986 – in German, unfortunately – that has an article, "Philip Johnson's Glass House in New Canaan – Modern as Postmodern," by Michael Hesse. It states that the Glass House is really the beginning of postmodernism.

Do you agree with that?

Sure, it's classical. But I didn't know it. It's a good point. Well, that was my main theme in teaching at Yale, that you cannot not know history. And you still can't, but there's a sense of freedom now. I mean, in no classical building would you take the wall and bring it out like a tent as I am trying to do today in the visitors pavilion in New Canaan.

And the Saudi project? That design is so big it looks like you are back to a Texas scale again.

Yes, it's more fun. I love that skyscraper. Taller the better. What I did was to take a few hints from Islam, of course. The skyscraper was something I had in mind a long time, the shifting planes floating casually in the sun.

But that was a competition. We always thought that you did not enter competitions.

I don't. But what do architects do now? There are no exceptions anymore. No AT&T walking into your office and asking, "Would you like to build a building?" In Berlin, it's the law. You can't build buildings without a competition.

So you had to compete for your office building there?

No, I got an exception there because I told them I wouldn't. Everybody else did.

In the Saudi Arabia project, who was your toughest competition?

Norman Foster, who won the competition. As for the tower, the reason I went in for it is I got this idea. In Saudi everything is solid against the sun. The planes that face the south and the east are all solid. The other planes are all glass, but they're all independent, and they tip and they wave. They just look like great planes hanging on the structure.

When you finished the design, did you think the tower would be a surprise for them?

Yes, I thought it would be a shock.

Are you making any progress on the chapel at the University of St. Thomas in Houston?

Oh, they haven't called me lately, because they haven't quite got enough money, but everybody likes it. That project is two or three years old.

Since you did it a while ago and it's not built yet, do you feel a desire to make modifications or change it?

I haven't faced that. I will. If they go ahead and build, I will certainly change it.

So nothing is complete until the day you start building?

It won't be over 'til the fat lady sings.

What happened to your project for the law school building at the University of Houston?

In the law school building, I took a chance. I felt that if I shredded the needs of the law school, I could do an interesting cluster, or grouping, of buildings. If I shredded the functional requirements into an auditorium, a study, and a library – if I made these into separate, little units – I could make sort of a village out of it that would be more interesting to use than a regular law school. So I combined that notion with my love, at the time, of Malevich, in order to make sort of a neo-constructivist design.

You would call that neo-constructivist, not "deconstructivist"?

No, it was constructivist. But it was new. By using a "Walk of the Law," as I called it, I created a covered way – more like a Roman road than anything – that would hold things together and off of which the buildings would be placed. I say "buildings," because the auditorium was a whole building, and then the two classrooms made up another building. The library was the third. They all had strange angles and were part of the village scheme. The effect was stunning. It was a little more expensive, of course, than the cheapest way to build. And the faculty didn't like it because they might have to walk outdoors for two minutes to go from one classroom to another. It got canceled. But I'm crazy about it.

Your architecture is very sculptural. Do you ever have a desire just to do sculpture, as opposed to doing architecture?

No, I'm not interested in small objects and sculpture. I'm interested in architecture.

UNIVERSITY OF ST. THOMAS PROPOSED CHAPEL

Do you see a separation between architecture and art, or are they one in the same?

Well, it has been defined that way: "Architecture is sculpture that is inhabited."

But there are people who argue against that. It's almost offensive to them to think of architecture as sculpture that is inhabited.

Both are right. To think of architecture as identical to sculpture is all wrong because of the question of scale. The building I'm doing now in New Canaan, I suspect, is going to be very peculiar, not as beautiful as I would like, because of the scale.

Because it's too small or too big?

It's too small. Every time I put a little figure in the model, I start laughing. If I make the figure about three-quarters scale, you sort of sigh with relief. Well, what does that mean for the finished building? Is this a toy or what? So that's the big thing about architecture versus sculpture, the scale of the human body. Now there is such a thing as sculpture that is large enough to get into. Well, I'm not so sure it makes any difference what words we use. The trouble is that I don't want to do sculpture *as* sculpture. I mean, if I did, if I twisted shapes and warped them like those in a salt shaker, it wouldn't be right, because a salt shaker depends on the feel of the fingers, as Michael Graves well understood, with his wonderful small objects. I think designing architecture and decorative objects are different arts.

In the law school buildings, I took a chance. I felt that if I shredded the needs of the law school, I could do an interesting cluster of buildings.

The interior is so important in the new pavilion in New Canaan. That's what I'm really most fascinated about there. What's it going to be like to have the corner of the room lean off 20-feet high when you're under a 10-foot high ceiling and standing straight up? I've been in some of Peter Eisenman's rooms in Japan where all six sides are warped. Of course, I find this sensation fantastically pleasant. But then I like that slight feeling of safe danger. Slightly unbalanced. Not quite dizzying, but toward that.

In all my buildings, I always try to get a little feeling of something that's slightly different. For example, the inside scale of the Glass House is different from the outside. "Am I indoors," as Frank Lloyd Wright said, "or am I out?" Well, that kind of ques-

UNIVERSITY OF HOUSTON LAW SCHOOL MODEL

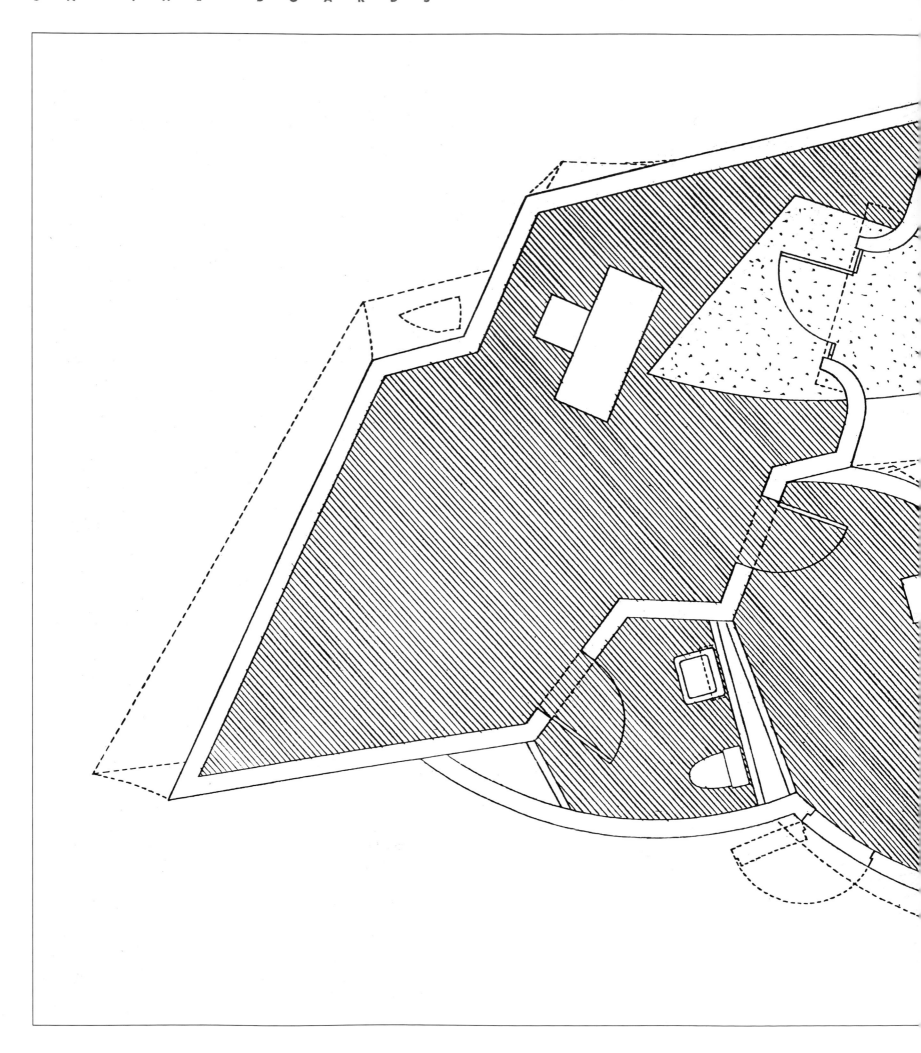

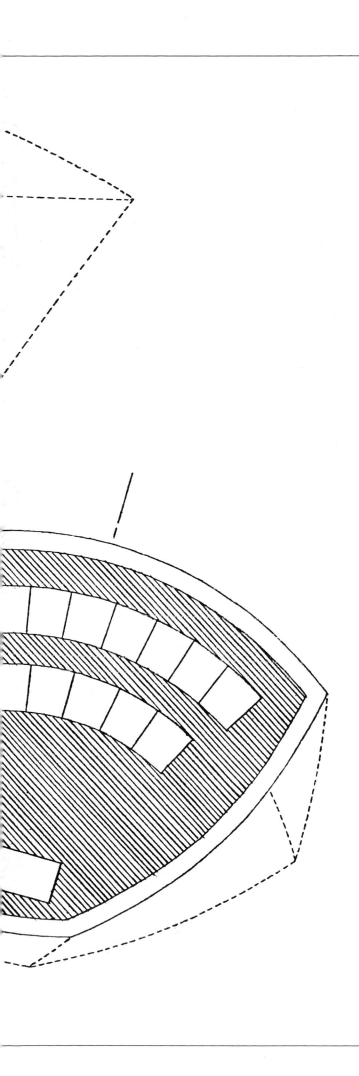

tion – the fact that anybody could ask a question like that – is a good thing.

I'm interested in the change of scale and the effect on the psyche. Like going up in the Lincoln Kirstein Tower. Most people don't make it all the way up, and that's wonderful. The fact that they turned around is a memory they'll always have, more than if I just had built a monument to look at, like a pyramid.

Because you interact with it?

Yes. It's unease, or semi-unease. It's hard to say. Well, it's titillation. Like the little bridge at the Glass House. I don't know anybody that couldn't get across the little bridge in New Canaan. But it was conceivable to me, anyhow, that since the bridge waves, an old lady might say, "George, hang on to me because the bridge is too narrow!" But I don't know how much that has to do with architecture. Because when you step into Chartres Cathedral, you get nothing but wonder. There's no feeling of danger, no feeling of unease, no visceral change.

There's another thing about architecture versus sculpture. A Brancusi bird is a Brancusi bird is a Brancusi bird. He made them in different sizes, with different materials, but it never changed. But architecture, if you build it at a different scale, is an entirely different experience. So sculpture can never reach architecture's proportions. In architecture, the feeling of the interior is a thing you always keep in mind. You can't think of a facade without thinking, "Will that be correct inside?" This kind of sculptural work I'm doing now is extremely tricky.

But you still think of it, of course, as architecture.

I do. Of course, there is a very close relation today between the two, especially in Frank Stella's sculpture and architecture.

Is it difficult to begin as a sculptor and move into architecture?

Michelangelo began as a sculptor. Bernini too.

Back then it was all mixed together.

I think that's possible again. You can be a tectonic architect and build beautiful bridges, as Santiago Calatrava does. Or you can start, as Frank Stella does, with shapes. But then somehow it's got to develop into an architecture, and that's what Frank Gehry is doing very well. It's a very interesting period to be alive.

If you could have anyone from the twentieth century design a house for you, whom would you choose?

I think Corbu. Because he was the most amenable to beautiful shapes that are new. When he used his head, like at Ronchamp, he was the most original. Mies would have just given me a thing about geometry that he had in his mind.

Acknowledgments

We first offer our gratitude to Philip Johnson for his generous and patient participation in this book. Also, we thank David Whitney for his excellent editorial assistance and contribution of photographs and illustrations. The office of Philip Johnson Architects has been consistently helpful throughout this project. In particular, we appreciate the tireless assistance of Aaron McDonald and Debby Green.

We commend our production and editorial team in Cambridge, Massachusetts. Kristen Langdon, Catherine Olofson, and Katherine Andrews worked brilliantly under demanding time constraints. Also, we applaud the fine transcription work of Connie Procaccini and the staff of Mulberry Studios.

Finally, this book is the product of a partnership between the authors and the people of Rizzoli. Our editor, David Morton, has been supportive from the earliest days of this project. We thank Judith Joseph, Rizzoli's president, who has shown great interest in making this book a reality. Our thanks to Elizabeth White, managing editor, and Andrea Monfried, associate editor, who have handled the production of the book.

The following individuals have also made major contributions to this book. We apologize for any inadvertent omissions.

Architectural Rendering: Emil Hoogendoorn

Avery Architectural and Fine Arts Library, Columbia University: Janet Parks, Daniel R. Kany

Boston Athenaeum: Rodney Armstrong, Catherine Slautterback, Sally Pierce

Canadian Centre for Architecture: Phyllis Lambert, Howard Shubert, Angela Forster, Maurice Boucher

Commissioned Photography: Nora Feller, Greg Gorman, Richard Payne

Hines Interests Limited Partnership: Gerald D. Hines, Louis S. Sklar, Stephen Ash, Joel D. Bracewell, Gary K. Johnson, Ann Kifer, Julie Mathis, Ben Quinton, John Williams

Harvard University: Neil Levine, Peter G. Rowe

Houston Chronicle: Ann Holmes

Massachusetts Institute of Technology: Lois Craig

The Museum of Modern Art, Archives: Rona Roob, Apphia Loo; **Department of Architecture and Design:** Peter Reed

Sony Music Entertainment, Inc.: Suzanne Satriano

Typographic House: Tom Delgiacco, Jack Tobin

And the other individuals who have provided various acts of generosity and support: Lee A. Daniels, Tom Dyja, Kathleen Economou, Michael Friedman, Garcia, Jeffrey L. Graubart, Stephen A. Greyser, Amy L. Halliday, A. Stover Jenkins, Herbert and Helene Lewis, David Mohney, John G. H. Oakes, Jerome A. Perles, Harold A. Pollman, Donald Porter, Rob Robinson, Marcia Sherrill, Elliot Stultz, Laurence H. Tribe, Jeannette S. Warner

Selected Bibliography

Beneš, Mirka. "Inventing a Modern Sculpture Garden at the Museum of Modern Art, New York." *Landscape Journal* 13, no. 1 (Spring 1994), 1-20.

The Charlottesville Tapes: Transcripts of the Conference Held at the University of Virginia School of Architecture, Charlottesville, Virginia, November 12 and 13, 1982. New York: Rizzoli, 1985.

Choisy, Auguste. *Histoire de l'architecture.* Paris: Gauthier-Villars, 1899.

"Design for Central Library Building Addition Approved." *BPL News,* Boston Public Library, March 1967, 1.

Goldberger, Paul. "The New American Skyscraper." *The New York Times Magazine,* November 8, 1981.

———. "80's Design: Wallowing in Opulence and Luxury." *The New York Times,* November 11, 1988, sec. 2.

Hesse, Michael. *Philip Johnsons Glashaus in New Canaan – Modern als Post-Moderne in Wie Eindeutig ist ein Kunstwerk?* Edited by Max Imdahl. Cologne: DuMont, 1986.

Heyer, Paul. "Philip Johnson." In *Architects on Architecture: New Directions in America.* New York: Van Nostrand Reinhold, 1993.

Hitchcock, Henry-Russell, and Philip Johnson. *The International Style: Architecture Since 1922.* New York: W. W. Norton & Company, 1966.

Hughes, Robert. "The Duke of Xanadu at Home." *Time,* October 26, 1970. Excerpted in Whitney and Kipnis, *Philip Johnson: The Glass House.*

Huxtable, Ada Louise. *Kicked a Building Lately?* New York: Quadrangle/The New York Times Book Co., 1967.

Jacobus, John M., Jr. *Philip Johnson.* George Braziller, Inc., 1962.

Johnson/Burgee: Architecture. Text by Nory Miller. Photographs by Richard Payne. New York: Random House, 1979.

Johnson, Philip. *Mies van der Rohe.* New York: The Museum of Modern Art, 1947.

———. *Philip Johnson: Architecture 1949-1965.* Introduction by Henry-Russell Hitchcock. New York: Holt, Rinehart and Winston, 1966.

Pacelle, Mitchell. "Noted Architects' Firm Falls Apart in Fight Over Control, Clients." *The Wall Street Journal,* September 2, 1992.

Philip Johnson/John Burgee: Architecture 1979-1985. Introduction by Carleton Knight III. New York: Rizzoli, 1985.

Philip Johnson: Processes. The Glass House, 1949, and the AT&T Corporate Headquarters, 1978. Catalogue 9, September 12 to October 31, 1978. Preface by Craig Owens. Introduction by Giorgio Ciucci. With two essays by Kenneth Frampton. New York: The Institute for Architecture and Urban Studies, 1978.

Philip Johnson Writings. Foreword by Vincent Scully. Introduction by Peter Eisenman. Commentary by Robert A. M. Stern. New York: Oxford University Press, 1979.

Sitte, Camillo. *The Art of Building Cities: City Building According to Its Artistic Fundamentals.* Translated by Charles Stewart. New York: Reinhold Publishing Corp., 1945.

Stern, Robert A. M., Gregory Gilmartin, and Thomas Mellins. *New York 1930: Architecture and Urbanism Between the Two World Wars.* New York: Rizzoli, 1987.

Tallmadge, Thomas Eddy. *Story of Architecture in America.* New York: W. W. Norton & Company, 1927.

Tomkins, Calvin. "Profiles: Forms Under Light." *The New Yorker,* May 23, 1977, pp. 43-80.

Whitney, David, and Jeffrey Kipnis, eds. *Philip Johnson: The Glass House.* New York: Pantheon Books, 1993.

The collected papers of Philip Johnson are maintained by the Archives of The Museum of Modern Art.

Index

Illustration Credits

Numbers refer to page numbers.